VADE MECUM

· ·

FORTY YEARS IN THEATRE'S HOTSPOTS

· ·

Rupert Rhymes

Cover photograph © Chris Arthur

Design, typesetting and publishing by UK Book Publishing

www.ukbookpublishing.com

ISBN: 978-1-916572-39-3

This account of my career is dedicated to the memory of two people who played important parts in it and gave me invaluable inspiration: Stephen Arlen, a great man of the theatre who presided over what really was our national opera company in the 1960s, and Yolande Bird, without whose determination our national theatre would not have opened in 1963.

CONTENTS

Notre rôle c'est de mettre un peu d'art
dans la vie et de vie dans l'art

Unattributed quotation seen on the wall of
Maison de la culture, Mulhouse

[Pearle conference, Basel, 1996]

VADE MECUM
- BY WAY OF INTRODUCTION

I was certainly never a great Latin expert (as my need to repeat Latin prelims at Oxford showed) but I always remembered the exhortation of my first Latin master to 'write it down, boy, in your *vade mecum*' – this being a particular exercise book with a pink cover where Latin words which had caused particular learning problems should be entered. This notebook was supposed to be kept to hand and used as a reference source – 'come with me.' This command to 'write it down, boy' was oft repeated and became something of a joke. How I wish looking back over my career I had followed that advice and made more notes. Peter Hall's diary-keeping in the challenging days of the National Theatre's industrial strife is much to be admired.

So come with me through some recollections and memories (helped by just a few notes made indiscriminately along the way) of what I consider to have been an enjoyable and, on occasions, challenging and certainly interesting, life in and around the theatre world. I have experienced many wedding reception speeches but the one which struck me as most appropriate was the one which exhorted the newlyweds to have 'an interesting life'. I certainly feel that has been my good fortune - though at times Sue and I have thought and called it many other things …

The family home at Kensington Place in Bath

GROWING UP IN BATH

. . . .

y mother always claimed I was born when the first bombs were dropped on Bath. Since the disastrous bombing of Bath was in 1942 as part of the Baedeker raids and I arrived on the scene in 1940 I suspect she was recalling one of the early air raid alerts at the time of Dunkirk. I was probably the result of my parents' sense of relief after Chamberlain assured the nation of 'peace in our time' after his Munich meeting with Hitler. As my two brothers, Trevor and Roy, were aged 13 and 11 I suspect my arrival must have caused something of a disturbance in the household but they were not around a great deal as I grew up: my eldest brother, Trevor, joined the British Army in India when he left school, returning at Partition and then training as a teacher, eventually joining the staff of the school he had once attended as pupil. My other brother, Roy, started farming with my Uncle Bob directly he was released from school – much to the disgust of my father, both because of the association with his brother-in-law and Roy's reluctance to attend agricultural college.

With brothers Trevor (left) and Roy (right) trying to look happy at the arrival of the new member of the family

I remember very little of my early days – a vague recollection of sheltering under the stairs when bombs were dropped on Bath otherwise little other than interminable journeys to the grocer. Although we had quite a good selection of local shops very near where we lived towards the edge of the city (those were the days when you could find a post office, butcher, baker and almost a candlestick maker in every community!) my mother made regular trips (entailing quite a long walk) to a general grocers on the edge of the historic part of the city. These trips stuck in my memory mainly because the shop was across the pavement from a bombed ruin, the Assembly Rooms. As I sat on a high stool and my mother spelt out items for the grocer to go around the store, collect and pack very carefully in her shopping bags, I was fascinated by the building I saw through the shop window with vegetation poking out of the roof. I gradually picked up stories of what it had been and how in ages past Bathonians had entertained themselves with card games and balls after they had taken the waters: the Assembly Rooms. Across the road there was another bomb site which still bore evidence of its role as Hotel Regina (I later learned this had been the scene of a number of fatal casualties in the '42 blitz).

Apart from the shopping at the grocers I vaguely recall visits to the grand buildings in the city centre whose functions were far removed from their original purpose – something to do with ration books in enormous rooms in a house in Great Pulteney Street and for something else 'official' (as my mother responded to my complaints of being dragged around such depressing places) in a maze of rooms which I learned after its demolition had been one of the historic hotels in the city centre, the Grand Pump Room Hotel. Around the city at this time there were numerous bomb sites and it was only at the time of the Festival of Britain in 1951 that there was a real drive to make these more presentable with flower beds and the like, since rebuilding (and more destruction) had to wait.

Carefully posed studio photo sent to Trevor in India 1946.
Left-to-right: my father, self, brother Roy and my mother

Perhaps the views from the grocer's window started my interest in the Georgian architecture of Bath. This was certainly fuelled when after my maternal grandmother's death in 1954 my parents decided that life would be easier in a flat and we moved into part of what had been my paternal grandfather's house, a five storey Georgian terrace house in Kensington Place next door to an old chapel on the main road into Bath from London. Kensington Place was designed by the architect John Palmer (there was also at the same period a John Palmer reforming the Bath theatre) and originally intended to be one side of a development like Queen Square in the centre of town - but the building boom was coming to an end by the time Kensington was completed in 1795.

My grandfather had bought the house in 1901 and I think let 'rooms' in much the same way as had been the case in Georgian times. By the time I knew the house it had suffered from the houses next door being razed in the blitz and repairs being made by the War Damage Commission with limited materials and certainly limited professional skills. It had a certain fascination for me when we moved there as it was next door to what had been a chapel and which was to feature in my youth employment.

As our few excursions only took in Bristol other than the seaside at Weston-super-Mare or boring (its pier had no slot machines!) Clevedon, it was some while before I realised there were also places built of brick... My father was keen on a bargain so when there was a cheap day excursion ticket to be had on the railway he booked up. One or two of these were to Bournemouth on the South Coast, so more chance of seeing the sea than at Weston on the Bristol Channel. The journey was via the Somerset and Dorset rail route so we passed on the way out of Bath the spot where we would come to live many years later

Another early memory relates to my very first day at school and the fact that I was given a piece of paper with a message from the King … I think this was the announcement of the end of WWII, Summer 1945. Contrary to my later magpie instincts, that piece of paper sadly did not get kept. My first classes were in the primary forms of Bath High School, part of the Girls' Public Day School Trust a part of which our daughter attended in London many years later. It took a little while to live down that my early education was in a girls' school!

My first dramatic role aged 9. I am on the far right enjoying wearing the family top hat. I think we are all holding copies of the (French) play, the title of which is long forgotten.

After primary school I moved on to the same grammar school in Bath as my brothers, father and grandfather had attended, King Edward VI grammar school, founded 1552. The Junior School was then housed in a Georgian terrace house which had at one time had been the headmaster's residence. This junior section of the school was headed by a master, Walter (Wally) Lewis, who was a veteran of WWI and was keen on retaining his military appellation of "Major" and also - as I and many contemporaries remembered – a believer in administering corporal punishment for behavioural and academic failings. There was a very splendid second form mistress, Miss Margaret Gardener, who each year produced a mini play in French – lasting all of fifteen minutes! I vaguely remember portraying a miserable Frenchman reprimanding an annoying child but most of all the chance to wear a family top hat, which brother Roy had also sported in his kindergarten play!

After 3 years I moved on to "Big School" - at that time housed in the Georgian building in the centre of the city which it had occupied since 1754. One of its most memorable features, and that which gave the building its name, was 'Big School' the large room where teachers had originally taught pupils in groups around four desks set against the walls of this - by my time - rather strange space. It was the scene each morning for Assembly, a procedure where, after prayers led by the Headmaster, a duty prefect read out the name of each pupil to which he acknowledged his presence with 'adsum'. (The school also used the Latin 'salve' and 'valete' to note new boys and leavers in the school magazine!) We all then trooped out to the various classrooms spread around the classic building.

A view of the school playground with summer fair in progress, showing how limited we were for outside space

Looking back I am amazed that we all fitted in to these rooms but then classes numbered no more than 20/25. Senior forms (fifth form and the two sixth forms) were housed next door in what had originally been the local parish school and then served as government offices during the war. They were reached by a passageway which necessitated a short walk in the open - distinctly unpleasant in the winter months. This building is now long gone – under a car park.

It is difficult to imagine how a prestigious grammar school operated in the space between the main shopping streets of the city. The only outdoor space was a tarmacked playground, overlooked by the backs of the premises whose fronts were the prestigious Milsom Street. One wall of this playground had a number of names carved on it and it wasn't until later I learnt these had been professionally inscribed to record pupils' presence, a rather upmarket form of graffiti. Although we didn't realise this at the time, the poor accommodation was of great concern to the school's governing body and more importantly the education authorities. Although the school had good academic results the facilities were well below those of comparable schools around the city so there was constant reference to the need for a 'new school' – which was achieved as I was leaving though not exactly with a 'new build'

*As a newly promoted corporal in the school's CCF
with the British Army of the Rhine in Germany*

As well as space for letting off steam in break periods
the playground also provided the parade ground for CCF
(Combined Cadet Force) parades. This was commanded
by the English master Bill Currie ("my name's Currie and
I'm hot stuff" being his opening line and indicative of his
approach...) who had served in the parachute regiment
and wore his regimental beret whenever he could. His
predecessor as CO was also on the staff: Colonel McGee
who taught chemistry and had served in WW1. In my time
(the cold war and the nuclear threat were considered very
real) the cadet force was popular with the majority of pupils
(it wasn't obligatory) but sadly lacked the band which had
existed in my two brothers' time. Just as well since the one

musical activity in the timetable was a weekly session of 'music' (lasting until the fourth form) which amounted to a session of rather unstructured 'singing', not I am afraid with any reference to musical heritage. Things did improve and by the time Bill Bailey was a pupil he was able to sit the A level music exam. Although my mother signed me up for private piano lessons for a while I am afraid I never excelled in any way in this direction, again in contrast to my brothers both of whom were accomplished pianists (and sang in the church choir).

Even if there wasn't a band we did have two cadet force trips to Germany staying with units of BAOR (British Army of the Rhine) – my very first trips abroad. I remember being struck on the first of these by the heavily damaged stations in Germany as we passed through on the lengthy train journey (after crossing the North Sea in a very basic troop ship) from the Hook of Holland to Detmold where we stayed with the IXth Royal Lancers in what had apparently been a rather prestigious barracks. Besides visits to see Centurion tanks out in the field on training exercises at Luneburg Heath (where the German surrender had been signed in 1945), followed by hair-raising rides in these unbearably cramped and noisy boxes on wheels, we also had some memorable sightseeing trips. One to Hamburg where one of the group went missing for several hours causing Currie more palpitations than the activities of the senior boys who were given free time to explore the city!

*As a proud 18 year old Senior Under
Officer in the Combined Cadet Force*

I suppose somebody in the army hierarchy could justify these visits – they were certainly appreciated by us! One outing took in Celle where we visited the Schloss and had a glimpse of its private theatre. Another recollection of this time was hearing on the forces radio at an evening meal in the NAAFI (canteen) that Dien Bien Phu had been lost by the French far away in SE Asia somewhere. Odd how you remember where these historic moments found you. I do remember heated discussion about the Suez invasion in our sixth form geography lessons – tenuous connections! Certainly, I can recall where I was when I heard that Kennedy had been assassinated - outside the Old Vic Stage Door; Sue and I watched the 1969 moon landing in an Oxfordshire country pub.

Another dramatic role – as Lord Loam
in the Admirable Crichton, aged 15

Apart from the German trip there were summer camps organised by the more go-ahead members of staff. The geography master, Rowland ('Roly') Dowson, a very active individual who had served in a Highland regiment during the war but was dead against the school's cadet force, was responsible for a number of camps with strenuous programmes (I suspect in opposition to the CCF activity). One of these to the Lake District resulted in the group being caught by a sudden storm and having to spend the night on a hillside. Newspaper headlines about this did not bring about the major investigations they would today! My only participation in such camps was that which went to a valley just outside Wooler in the Cheviots and which convinced me that I was not a particularly energetic type! By contrast the history master, Donald (Don) Mackay, ran an altogether more relaxed operation for several years to the Channel Islands. He and Dowson were two of the younger members of staff and whilst Dowson had seen military service Mackay had not for medical reasons.

Mackay's brother was an actor, Angus, who was a member of the Bristol Old Vic company in the late forties and eventually married Dorothy Reynolds. I heard a lot about these two and enjoyed visits to the musicals with music by Julian Slade and words by Dorothy which were something of an end of season romp at the Bristol Old Vic. Many years later in my Coliseum days I remember being invited to join Dorothy and Angus for lunch in the atmospheric Beottys in St Martin's Lane but I never got to know them well, whereas Donald and his wife, Joan, became family friends. When Sue and I bought our first house in Clapham we found that we were in an adjacent street to Dorothy and Angus. The story was that their curtains were made from the Vaudeville house curtains which had been replaced on the success of the run of "Salad Days", transferred from Bristol Old Vic.

Whilst the school cadet force was voluntary, games were obligatory one afternoon a week and involved a bus journey to playing fields away on the edge of the city. The general expectation was that – one day – the school would move to a new building on the edge of these fields overlooking the Avon valley. In my last year at school events took a dramatic turn when the Governors took advantage of the closing of a small private school in its own grounds on the edge of the city, St Christopher's, and decided to purchase the site and move the school and implement long overdue reforms and expansion (a second stream in each year!) The move to new premises happened after my time and the Junior School used the Broad Street premises in the city until a new building was completed in 1990 by which time our son was a pupil and took part in the 'pageant' organiscd by my brother, Trevor, to mark the movc. An activity which enabled him to indulge both his military and theatrical passions!

As a sixth former (and deputy Head Prefect, also the Senior Under Officer in the CCF!) I got very much involved in the appeal set up to raise funds for the move. There was something satisfying about the challenge of doing something different – preparing mailings and planning events far outside the normal run of things as part of a fundraising campaign. Perhaps this was a foretaste of the future. The governors sold land adjoining the playing fields for development and various properties in the city which had been part of the school's endowment thanks to Henry VIII – proceeds of the dissolution of Bath Priory. There was still a substantial amount to raise. This was in the late 50s in the days well before development offices were the norm. Our Headmaster, HM Porter (Harry) was certainly not one for too much contact with parents but was persuaded to accept an appeal committee with active parent participation.

For some years at the end of the summer term there had been a 'Hobbies Exhibition' in various parts of the school building giving parents the opportunity of wandering through decorated classrooms to marvel at various examples of the activities of their beloved offspring on show. It now seems unbelievable but this was the only time when parents came into the building and had contact with staff – parents' evenings were NOT on the agenda in my day (so it was an entirely new experience when I was involved as a parent myself!) I recall mounting two displays for these exhibitions one quite adventurous on Bath and Postal History which entailed arranging the loan of a painting from the city council's collection. Not something which would even be contemplated these days.

As part of the fundraising for the school's move the annual hobbies exhibition was adapted in my last year into a major summer fair providing more experience for this budding organiser. We thought we did rather well with our fund raising efforts but I am afraid there was still a large amount to be found so it was good that one of the school's governors was manager of a local bank and able to play a significant part in arranging the finance for the school to move in the year after my departure.

There was a general expectation that all pupils who reached the sixth form would try for university places. Our headmaster had his English degree from Cambridge and he encouraged us all to apply first of all to the Oxford and Cambridge colleges before trying for the 'red brick' establishments as Porter described them. By now my brother Trevor had married Rosamund, a graduate of Bristol University, and I suspect my mother would have preferred me to go there rather than distant places - heaven knows what she would have made of a place at St Andrew's! Rosamund was a brilliant English teacher and often clarified what Currie had glossed over in English lessons

There were some colleges which held common entrance exams but certainly not the unified system of later years. I sat quite a few of these exams very often in cold and rather miserable Oxford premises, having for some reason decided I liked the sound of Oxford more than Cambridge. At the start of the spring term in 1959 I received the results of a scholarship exam I had sat before Christmas for Magdalen College. The letter (from AJP Taylor) advised that I hadn't got any scholarship but could take up a commoner's place – in other words I was in if I paid! Not quite so daunting as it sounds because in those halcyon days there was the possibility of securing a maintenance grant from one's local authority, which thankfully I did. There would have been no way my parents could have financed my time at Oxford.

After a lengthy summer job as a furniture removal porter - the firm using the chapel next to home as their store meant little travelling time! - I set off for the dreaming spires of Oxford to take up my study of Modern History in the wonderful surroundings of Magdalen College - the only KES pupil, I think, to achieve an Oxford place that year. History had been my favourite and best subject for many years so it was a natural choice.

I think I worked as a furniture remover and auction porter until quite close to the date for 'going up' to Oxford.

Gap years and the like were not common at this time and I was somewhat anxious about finance never having had to balance my own budget before. I knew there was no spare cash as far as my parents were concerned: my father worked as a traveller for a well-established local bacon curers and sausage manufacturer before succumbing to TB during my time at Oxford.

Indeed life away from home in Bath would be an entirely new experience. I had never boarded or spent extended periods away from home and as both brothers had not been around for many years I suppose I was something of an only child. I was steeped in the rather cosy atmosphere of the city which had not yet achieved its university status or come alive except for the ten days of its arts festival, then under the title of The Bath Assembly attempting to recall its Georgian heyday.

I had no family experience to call on; Trevor didn't offer much comment about his teacher training at Loughborough and Roy had already consigned me to the 'arty lot'. My father's further education had been in the university of life after school!

What would Oxford be like? Life was going to be very different.

THE
DREAMING SPIRES

Magdalen College, Oxford

In early days Magdalen life was rather daunting. Because the college had decided to accept both those straight from school and those who had completed National Service which had just ended, accommodation in college was in short supply. So my first year was spent in digs in Iffley Road with daily bicycle commutes into Magdalen. Gradually I got to know some like-minded souls - with an interest in drama - and formed friendships which have lasted through the years. My friends came from a variety of backgrounds, this being one of the merits of Magdalen despite it being an 'actually' college. (When asked your college: 'well, **actually**, Magdalen or the House or BNC.') I suppose it may also have been the mix of ex National Service with those straight from school which made one oblivious of which school one had attended. Yes, there were many from Eton and the like and indeed some non-white faces but it wasn't anything which really entered into discussion. (Times change: Magdalen like others now looks carefully at the 'social mix' of its intake each year.) In my second year I moved into college and occupied rather better rooms than would have been available in my first year (a separate bedroom, though hot and cold running water would come only in my third year).

I suppose, my involvement with theatre really began at Oxford. I had acted in school plays – or rather walked on or carried a spear - until the boy playing Gremio in *The Taming of the Shrew* fell ill at the last moment. For this production I had volunteered as a stage manager/dogsbody and had attended all rehearsals so it was felt that I could at least read the script and make the right moves. Once in the swing of things I rather enjoyed myself and apparently pulled off an acceptable performance without too much reference to the script. In following years I gave, according to reviews, an 'admirable Crichton' in Barrie's play but a 'not so convincing Kent' in *King Lear.* Armed with these 'achievements' I was an early subscriber to OUDS at the Freshers' Fair at Oxford in 1959 – in those days a melee of tables and posters in the town hall when the officials of the university's various clubs and societies endeavoured to sign up as much new blood as possible.

There was an air of expectation at that time in the country. Harold Macmillan had convinced the electorate that they'd never had it so good and been rewarded with an election victory for the Tory party which a few years earlier, after the disaster of the Suez invasion, would have been thought impossible. There were the inevitable political campaigners amongst my contemporaries, (many joined the Aldermaston CND marches I recall) but many were keen on the theatre. There was certainly a fair amount of live theatre on offer at the two professional theatres which were in operation: a large commercial theatre, the New Theatre, which boasted in large letters that it was 'England's finest theatre', the justification for which escaped us. It housed visiting, large scale shows and was managed in a traditional way by the Dorrill family. The smaller Playhouse was home to the Meadow Players who under Frank Hauser's direction offered us some notable productions – *A Passage to India* stands out from the offerings in early days. There were gaps in the schedule when the Playhouse was available to amateur and university companies such as the OUDS (Oxford University Dramatic Society).

Having signed up as a member of OUDS at the Freshers' Fair, I thought it a positive sign that my audition secured me a part in the society's Hilary (i.e. Spring) Term major production of *Measure for Measure*, to be jointly directed by a Merton don, Merlin Thomas, and the President of OUDS, Ken Loach. The idea apparently being that one would direct the comedy scenes and the other the tragedy but there was uncertainty as to which was which ...

*Mucking about post Finals, L-R Paul Rayment,
John Richards, self, Peter Fiddick*

The machinations of university theatre gradually became clear: a good actor who could also promote himself (yes, male dominated - female roles were taken by *guest* female undergraduates - only a few years previously OUDS had engaged professional actresses!) would be elected as President of OUDS or its rival ETC (Experimental Theatre Club, younger in foundation) for a year. The OUDS presidential year ran from elections around the Annual Dinner in Hilary Term leading up to the major production in that term in the following academic year. I reckoned this gave the new president sufficient time to decide on the play and the part he wanted to play'. It also provided time for him to establish himself and persuade the committee to adopt his choice.

My part in the *Measure* production turned out to be 'first officer,' a classic spear carrier if ever there was one! At the first walk through I performed in such a way that Loach commented that I needn't emulate Dixon of Dock Green (the BBC TV police soap of the time). The production eventually came together but didn't log up great reviews, hopefully unconnected with my participation. I duly reported on my Oxford stage debut to my parents who encouraged me not to get 'too involved'. Trevor (an actor whether teaching or actively involved with amateur theatricals!) duly came with Rosamund and witnessed a performance. No great enthusiasm shown!

I made a number of friends as a result of involvement with *Measure* including a fellow historian at Magdalen, Neil Stacy whose ability on stage showed just what my portrayal of elderly characters in school plays had lacked! We became good friends and Neil played a significant part in my later involvement with the business side of university theatre. It had become the practice for the OUDS major production to tour in the Easter vacation to a circuit of French theatres set up by Merlin Thomas, a modern languages don at Merton and one of the society's senior members (all societies had dons in such roles – I suppose a way of keeping an eye on undergraduate activities). I had no desire to join the *Measure* French tour, however, largely because I needed to restore my bank balance with a holiday job rather than spend cash on a trip with very much more theatrically committed individuals (or so I believed).

For my holiday employment I returned to my role as a furniture remover which had the added advantage of keeping me fit . My role gradually expanded into that of an auction room porter. As mentioned, our home in Bath was next door to what had been built as a proprietary chapel. Originally this would have meant pews could be rented in a small chapel which was subsidiary to the parish church and the income providing support; good preacher, good return just like the theatre! During WWII the chapel had become a furniture store the owners of which (Berry, Powell & Shackell) operated one of the city's auction rooms in the former General Post Office. As a result of my several vacation employments I learnt a lot about loading vans with three piece suites (remember those?) and how auctions worked (reserve prices and local bids) with some rather sad experiences of clearing grand houses in the city which had survived the war but were destined not to survive 'redevelopment'. The head of the firm occasionally ran the auctions himself exchanging enjoyable banter with the public. His daughter, Mary Berry, certainly went on to make her mark as a television personality!

Despite my first dubious experience of Oxford theatre the interest remained and so my first summer term found me attending a number of productions which various bodies mounted in a variety of locations in the city. In college I took an interest in the activities of Magdalen Players – play readings, discussions and meetings about a future production by the group.

We were very fortunate in having as the head (President) of Magdalen, Tom Boase, who besides being no mean art historian was a great theatre lover. In our early terms Boase was serving his turn as Vice Chancellor so had an opportunity of indulging in Oxford's unique brand of theatre whilst still finding the time for dinner parties in his lodgings which distinguished theatre personalities often attended. I am sure a fair amount of arm twisting of guests for college funds must have gone on but the President's role in my undergraduate days was not that of master fundraiser it was later to become.

Boase took a benign interest in Magdalen Players as well as all that happened in the wider Oxford theatre scene. To be fair I never met any of my contemporaries who didn't commend Boase for his ability to conduct a detailed conversation on any subject. Throughout my time at Oxford the *grande dame* of the professional theatre in Oxford was Elizabeth Sweeting who managed the Playhouse. Boase was a particular admirer of hers. I think it fair to say that it was Elizabeth (Liz) who really gave me the bug for theatre administration. After my limited acting experience with OUDS and mediocre activity in readings with Magdalen Players, I found myself more drawn to the organisation involved in production than to treading the boards. A throw-back to my school days of organising my fellow human beings, I suppose.

My first administrative 'break' was as publicity manager for the 1961 OUDS major production at the Playhouse, now under the banner of The University Theatre. The machinations whereby the Playhouse became the University's responsibility from the beginning of 1961 were lost on me at the time but later knowledge would reveal much about university personalities and politics. The important thing was that the OUDS major production of *Richard II* was to be the first university production in the university theatre. It was to be directed by Michael Croft, the director of the National Youth Theatre which had its origins in Croft's teaching at Alleyn's School in Dulwich a decade before. More significantly, my friend Neil had performed in Croft productions and it was probably Neil's comments to Croft which secured my place on the production team and, through lengthy, often alcohol filled sessions, gave me some useful theatre background.

My early experience of theatre pre-Oxford was limited. There were regular visits to the panto at the Theatre Royal in Bath ("The best in the West"), several visits to Bristol Old Vic (enjoying what was a particularly successful period) and some trips to Stratford (still then The Memorial Theatre). The London West End theatre was, however, a closed book so I was an eager listener to the accounts Croft gave of what went on there.

Publicity Manager for an OUDS major production sounds very grand. Actually it meant doing everything from designing the publicity, distributing posters and leaflets, contacting the press for stories and ads but above all making sure the budget wasn't overspent. I have forgotten what that was (but probably have a piece of paper somewhere with the details!) but the dread of overspending kept me on my toes in negotiating prices. I had no previous experience of such business (though my father, as a travelling salesman, was brilliant at mental arithmetic and adding up figures on an invoice) apart from that appeal activity in my latter days at school. Another Magdalen contemporary, Peter Fiddick, was the production's business manager so with contact in college we were able to keep abreast of what was happening very easily, although as Peter was in digs at this time it did mean he spent quite a few nights on my sofa in college. Pieces of paper and tangible receipts were necessary in those days. Peter had been in the RAF for National Service prior to Magdalen so certainly knew something about 'presentation'.

One story from a previous era made a lasting impression on me. I had a room in my second year on Kitchen Staircase at Magdalen (so named as it was tucked away close to the kitchens) and the services of a scout (Betnay) who had looked after Ken Tynan when resident as an undergraduate between 1945 and 48 in this part of college. 'Scout' perhaps needs a little explanation: my college accommodation was not *en suite* (very few were at that time) and one's scout brought hot water (bowl and ewer time!) in the early morning for washing (unless your outer door was shut for reasons best left unrecorded) and cleaned your room. Ken was a great exhibitionist and according to Betnay an early manifestation of this at Oxford was his success in booking the advertising hoardings all along the High Street for the beginning of a term – not to promote a production but simply to proclaim 'TYNAN!' Inspired by this story from my scout I determined to get *Richard* posters abundantly in evidence in shop windows in the High (as it was known – 'Street' was/is rarely added by the university fraternity) by the beginning of the term when *Richard* was to be mounted. With a great deal of footwork and glib talking I didn't know I was capable of, this was duly achieved.

Neil had on display in his rooms a collection of prints of English monarchs and one of Richard II provided the inspiration for my next foray into graphic design. I put together a leaflet with performance details which I persuaded a print shop to sponsor – in those days sponsorship was essentially just paid advertising in the form of editorial text. Unfortunately the Richard print didn't get returned to Neil until many years later by which time his series of prints had been framed without Richard in his correct historical place!

After a lot of hard work *Richard II* turned out to be a box office success but rather less so with the critics. There were those who felt OUDS had been served up just another version of the *Richard* production given by Croft's National Youth Theatre in the West End the year before but as far as I was concerned it was a good interpretation of a play I was familiar with from school days. I am not sure how much Croft intended to emphasise the effeminate nature of Richard and his relationship with his favourites but to the company it became the basis of a calypso, conceived by Ian McCullough (not directly involved as a cast member but a very active OUDS member). Ian's rendering of the refrain "Now who was the queen, was it Bushy, Bagot or Green" was widely enjoyed and quoted.

The calypso brought about my first encounter with Oxford 'censorship'. Since the Playhouse was the University Theatre, Liz Sweeting now reported to a board of 'curators' (a strange term but in line with other non-academic establishments the university ran). As a group of us involved with *Richard* (including one Michael Brunson) had felt the calypso would make a good fund raiser for Playhouse funds as an EP we set about a foray into the record industry. Even though this was the beginning of the swinging sixties there were rumblings amongst the Playhouse curators about the content of the EP. Liz duly summoned me and pointed out it was 'unfortunate' that I had not discussed the project with her in advance. Useful experience I suppose!

In the Easter vacation *Richard* followed previous practice and went on tour to France. This time I decided to join what was a notable company. I suppose everyone can look back to university days and pick out one or two contemporaries who made names for themselves in later years. Certainly this was the case with members of the *Richard* cast (this and later productions in my time certainly fostered some notable television newscasters). At Oxford the king was played by Richard Hampton who was a Youth Theatre stalwart and went on to deliver the very first words spoken in a National Theatre production (officer Bernardo in *Hamlet*, when NT opened at Old Vic). Peter Snow portrayed Northumberland

and gave early examples of his later television swingometer technique when delivering the bard's lines, while Gordon Honeycombe was the Bishop of Carlisle.

Richard Hampton, who was approaching finals, wanted to make up the study time which dramatic activity had eroded, so Richard Sherrington stepped up from Bolingbroke to play the king. Richard went on to a career with the British Council (sadly losing his life in a Comet crash) and later plied me with accounts of dramatic activity in a middle east posting where a borrowed sword for a production came with recent evidence of serious use! With limited scope for pure admin in the tour budget those like myself had to fill in as the soldiers and inevitable attendants whilst also undertaking admin duties. As Merlin Thomas - who had masterminded the previous seven tours - was not in attendance, the admin responsibilities fell to Peter Fiddick and myself during the two week tour.

After a night crossing to Rouen (more acceptable than my schoolboy troop ship crossing to Holland had been) the tour schedule started in a very utilitarian university building in Caen (which still bore the signs of its flattening during the war) then went on to the rather barn like Theatre des Celestins in Lyons before reaching a gem of a theatre in Versailles town. Many years later when visiting the restored theatre inside the palace, I was able to point out to Sue the theatre where I had actually trod the boards! In 1961 this was still very much the local town for SHAPE (Supreme Headquarters Allied Powers Europe) personnel who made up a large part of our audience. I doubt if at this stage of the tour our performances were an artistic triumph and probably only distantly related to the original Oxford version, but they delighted audiences and we all enjoyed splendid hospitality. I seem to remember some of us even managed to get transport in to sample the delights of Paris nightlife and somehow back again. All too soon the fun and games were over and we were back to Victoria via the delights of a boat train – flying would have been out of the question given cost in those days!

It will be realised from this account that theatre played a large part in my life at Oxford but it did not completely dominate in the way it did for some contemporaries. I am not sure how much of the real theatre world my friends and I took in, this was after all the period immediately after *Look Back in Anger* and happenings at the Royal Court were regularly in the news. The Sunday papers were avidly read in the JCR and the latest comments from Ken Tynan and Harold Hobson much discussed. Both these critics featured in my later life – Tynan as a senior figure at Olivier's National Theatre and Hobson as a member of the Society of London Theatre's Awards Panel.

Study involved lectures, tutorials and research in the various Oxford libraries. Lectures rarely had visual aids but I think this put an onus on those delivering to deliver their views in an arresting fashion. Some did, some didn't, and however prominent the latter's lectures were on recommended lists from tutors, the attendance was poor; in theatre terms, 'seats at all prices'.

Sally McLaren's poster for the OUDS production of
The Shoemaker's Holiday in 1961. Not sure there
was strict adherence to the dress code!

One don who could always get a full house even at 9 o'clock in the morning was AJP Taylor who had an ability to talk about his subject and hold your attention all through the hour. Though I found his later television series enjoyable the press did not - as one headline put it: <u>A</u>ll <u>J</u>aw and no

Pictures Taylor. I was very fortunate with my tutors and particularly enjoyed sessions with John Stoye who always demanded 'feeling' when you read your efforts on that week's set topic. My first year involved shared tutorials (as opposed to the traditional one-to-one with a tutor) because of the large intake of students (those who had been on National Service joining those straight from school). So Bevis Hillier and I shared such a tutorial where we offered our very different thoughts on early English history for an hour each week. Bevis certainly took an artistic route subsequently, becoming a renowned art historian, as well as writing a notable biography of John Betjeman.

My second summer at Oxford was extremely enjoyable – enhanced as I recall with mostly good weather. Magdalen Players decided that it was time once more to risk a production and we (yours truly being a committee member) had eventually settled on Ben Jonson's *Volpone* to be staged in the Grove at Magdalen. The Grove was the preserve of the college deer herd so that entailed negotiation with the don responsible for them (my tutor, Stoye), and clearance, of course, from the President. There was also the little matter of arranging the scaffolding for the seating. I think Boase was remarkably restrained when he wrote "They certainly put it across, though whether their version really represented the play is more open to question". Michael Beloff, reviewing the production in the undergraduate magazine *Isis,* concluded that "this performance, despite the gnats and the cold, is worth seeing above all for its enterprise". We more or less broke even. Enough said.

OUDS had invited David Webster to mount their major production that summer and Thomas Dekker's *The Shoemaker's Holiday* had been selected. At this time David was balancing his progress to the bar with appearances as police cadet Jamie in the *Dixon of Dock Green* TV series. He had been in the cast of a notable *Tamburlaine* whilst at Christ Church a couple of years earlier. From our first meeting David made it quite clear that he intended to create a theatrical event, and he set about making everything from set design to additional participants a talking point. Perhaps his greatest success in this direction was involving Christ Church and New College beagles who with their beaters delighted every audience with their ability to wander all over the set. The production was staged in Wadham College cloister and for the set Sally McClaren (the future Mrs Webster as well as a notable Royal Academy print maker) conceived a high level platform on the cloister roof with a sweeping staircase down to audience level - a set which also featured in Sally's very eye catching poster.

My role in all this was Business Manager, which meant controlling the finances whilst giving David all he wanted. There was many a headache balancing David's ideas with budget availability. Whilst the end result was not as earth shattering as David had hoped, we all had great fun and once again managed to avoid a disastrous financial result. The cast list included a number of players who would feature in the entertainment world in the years ahead. Christopher

Matthew, Oliver Davies (Ford came later for Equity reasons), Sam Walters, Michael Brunson, (one of many who found a serious role in television) and Sheridan Morley were all involved besides Neil Stacy who had become an OUDS regular (but surprisingly failed to become President). I think David even persuaded Dudley Moore to provide 'additional' musical material without incurring any cost.

Year 3 was supposed to be for hard academic work – which it certainly was without being totally devoid of theatre activity. By now I had become OUDS archivist which I felt gave me a certain status and excuse for continuing my organising activity. Michaelmas term saw my involvement with ETC's 25th anniversary production, *Peer Gynt,* as 'business consultant' (what arrogance!) and the experience of working with Sam Walters who certainly made his mark in years to come with his work at the Orange Tree in Richmond. In February 1962 OUDS mounted its 114th major production *Henry IV parts 1 & 2.* This was an unqualified artistic success created for the society by Peter Dews who had just made marvellous television of Shakespeare's history plays. It was decided that OUDS should support the Playhouse improvements £50,000 appeal, which had just been launched, with a gala performance of part 2. Yes, I got involved and delighted in the title of 'Gala Performance Manager'. More importantly, the cast was particularly notable for future star names, including one Michael Johnson (as Lancaster) who I would come across again at the National as Michael York.

ON TO A DIFFERENT LIFE – THE ALDWYCH AND THE WELLS

Sadler's Wells Theatre in the 1960s

All good things come to an end so apart from the horrors of finals (exams taken in white tie academic dress, producing a degree conferred in a formal ceremony in the Sheldonian Theatre) there was the need after a mostly delightful 3 years to address the future and find a job. Oxford's version of a careers advisory service in the 60s was the University Appointments Committee. The staff were, I am sure, brilliant at pointing to routes into regular career paths but theatre admin which I had decided was my metier, was not one of them. My adviser suggested that I should try for a job with one or other of the commercial television companies which had recently been established since I firmly ruled out applying for any of the BBC traineeships which were around and caught attention of many contemporaries. Perhaps it was the size of the BBC which put me off as I felt there would be little chance of much hands-on activity. There followed a stream of applications and even some interviews during the summer of '62 with TV companies such as Television Wales and West, and Southern - now consigned to history.

I had always intended to give myself a memorable adventure after Oxford and formed the plan with a friend from Magdalen, Brian Powell, also from the West Country, of driving to Portugal where an elderly relative of Brian's conveniently lived. Brian introduced me to sailing (at then little-known Padstow) and horse riding (briefly) and we got as far as investigating the purchase of an old Land Rover – I was very anxious to exercise my newly acquired driving licence - before the mounting estimate and my lack of success on the job front brought us round to realising the costs associated with a rail journey would be more achievable.

Our rail journey brought no particular hazardous encounters with the fascist regimes in Spain or Portugal itself. When we arrived in Oporto the long hours on third class wooden bench seats had certainly left an impression. India had recently taken over the Portuguese colony of Goa and I remember being told by some university students we met that 'Goa had gone away from us', the approved explanation from the Caetano regime! As we were visiting in September I had expected to find the climate much warmer than it was - Atlantic swimming was invigorating - but we did manage some interesting sightseeing. The old university town of Coimbra sticks in my memory as does one of the car journeys around Oporto when Brian's relative forgot his way and was confronted outside a government building by an armed guard who clearly meant business when he lowered his rifle to halt our progress.

After the interlude in Portugal job hunting became more urgent though it must be admitted with only limited prompting from my parents about the need to get a job and earn a living I had discussed with my contact at the Appointments Committee in Oxford the idea of something associated with theatre admin and now decided to concentrate on this approach. I wrote what must have been pretty naive letters to the managements I could identify from my regular reading of *The Stage* newspaper. Some of the replies I received were curtly polite, but one or two, whilst holding out little prospect of employment, invited me to come and have a chat when in London. I needed no excuse to follow these up and there followed a series of interviews with some of the greats and not so greats of the day who were to reappear in my later professional life. One trip, to the HM Tennent office at the Globe theatre, stands out in my memory because, after the journey up to the office eyrie in the smallest lift I had ever come across, there was a brief 'hello' from someone who I learnt was the great 'Binkie' Beaumont who had obviously mistaken me for someone he was expecting. I was quickly passed on to chat with general manager Bernard Gordon. It was only later that I gathered these offices had once been a flat used by the theatre manager and that such eyries existed in some other theatres until they had become rent producing office accommodation. Another interview was with Laurier Lister in the Laurence Olivier Productions offices but no sign of that great man – the street where those offices stood has now been obliterated by the Inn on the Park hotel.

There was also the experience of meeting Bernard Miles. In typical fashion Bernard had conceived the idea of getting money from a commercial company (I think Leverhulme - probably a way for them to get credit for a 'charitable' activity, way before such actions became strictly formulated) to cover the wages of employing someone to learn about theatre whilst working (all hours imaginable) at the new Mermaid theatre in the City of London. When I saw the ad for this I immediately applied. My interview coincided with a day when the remains of an ancient boat had been discovered in the mud at Puddle Dock alongside the Mermaid. The encounter with Bernard (in his muddy wellingtons) was brief but I went on to an enjoyable session with Pat Ide - a great theatre character who was ostensibly managing the Mermaid. Pat and I later reflected on this early encounter with different versions of the discussion! Nothing came of this by way of a job at the time but Pat certainly continued to feature in my theatre life until his death.

Summer 1962 had seen the opening of the Chichester Festival Theatre inspired by a local business man who had managed to secure Olivier's interest and who persuaded him to become its Director. Olivier's General Manager, Pieter Rogers, agreed to offer some career suggestions when I wrote to him. Another letter to another theatre hotspot at the time, Stratford upon Avon, brought an invitation for a chat (the 'in' expression it seemed) from Peter Hall's General Manager, Paddy Donnell. Paddy echoed the comments of Pieter Rogers and many of the other theatre people I had pestered with the Rhymes appeal, that if I was really serious about a career in theatre management I should spend some time in a box office. He volunteered to mention my name to his colleagues in London where the newly designated Royal Shakespeare Company had taken over the Aldwych Theatre. I remembered driving back home thinking about the contrast between a rather laid back Stratford and what I had seen of the intense activity of London theatreland and wondering if I would ever achieve a place in either; they both seemed so remote from life in Bath where there was absolutely no sign of the swinging sixties. Like many of my contemporaries I had had little contact with Oxford city life either, besides theatres, cinemas, cafes and bookshops, so I felt I really was on the threshold of 'the real world'.

I did hear from the Aldwych in the form of a letter from the theatre manager, Mick Orr, inviting me to attend an interview with the box office manager, Bill Shene, and himself. I duly presented myself at the Aldwych and having fought through a sizeable queue for the box office was asked to go up some obviously back stairs – uncarpeted - to a rather grand office looking out over the Aldwych itself. This I learnt during my interview was actually Peter Hall's office, but was being used as 'he is rarely here'. Years later it became the office of Michael Codron who certainly was regularly there.

It had been obvious to me from the lengthy queues downstairs that the box office was under considerable pressure from those wishing to see Paul Scofield in *King Lear* and enjoy *The Comedy of Errors* produced by Clifford Williams. In the course of my interview Messers Orr and Shene revealed that the pressure was considerable and the need for extra staff a priority. On the basis, I suppose, that with an Oxford degree (albeit in Modern History) I must be able to add up and be in reasonable command of the three 'Rs', I left with a job offer at £11 per week, to start as soon as possible. My father was horrified at the pay wondering what Oxford had done for me. Now I had to come up with somewhere to stay pdq.

I eventually found a bed - more precisely, a sofa - in the Kilburn flat of two Oxford friends and my box office career began. On first reporting to the Aldwych one morning in early September I was assigned to the Ladies toilet off the main foyer as my place of work except on matinee days; such was the pressure on space in the box office itself. In those days the box office was even smaller than it is today – and in those pre-computer times, filled with vast sacks of booking mail and walls lined with racks of ticket books. My job consisted of opening the multi-sized envelopes, checking there was a remittance within and then deciphering what the patron wanted. I soon realised that whoever had put the booking leaflet together had very little idea of how much space the average customer needed just to write the minimum request. Letters requesting tickets, meanwhile, could be unbelievably lengthy and still omit essential information. I soon got the hang of my allotted task and became quite attached to my cosy Ladies boudoir with a carpet pattern which was to become very familiar to me. I later discovered the extensive Stoll Moss theatre management had purchased vast amounts of the same carpet and furnished all theatres they controlled with it, regardless of surrounding décor.

Not only was there considerable post to be processed but from the moment the box office opened there was a queue snaking around the foyer and out around the corner on to Drury Lane. As I occasionally needed to refer to colleagues in the box office itself, I received curious looks when I emerged from behind the 'Ladies' door.

One of the experienced staff decided that I deserved rather more background to the world of London commercial theatre than my boss, an ultra-traditional box office manager, was willing to give. So it was that I learnt about 'long toms' (an analysis of the day's ticket sales), 'matured bookings', 'blueing in' and other mysteries of the time. In pre-computer days and apparently from the 1880s tickets consisted of several sections. Two were given or posted to the patron whilst a third was also drawn from the ticket book and set aside to be used for accounting purposes . Each day a clerk was assigned the task of sorting these by performance and price and then calculating their value resulting in the sum of money which had been taken from customers – 'the advance'. When this had been checked against cash received a large sheet, the 'plan', with numbers on it (one for each performance available for booking with the numbers representing the seats in the theatre) could be coloured in with a blue crayon to indicate that the sale had been accounted for, that is, 'matured'. If a booking had been made by post somehow the customer's name would be written on the plan, hopefully in such a fashion as to be legible in case of query. If the sale had been made to a patron at the box office window the tickets would be bracketed together to indicate a sale as a single, pair or otherwise.

Although it had disappeared from the London theatre scene by my time in the 60s I remember being told about the practice of one management which issued pencils which had a distinctive marking on their blunt ends. When a clerk made a ticket sale the plan would be stamped by the pencil end which had been inked on a stamp pad. Any sale could theoretically be traced back to the clerk who had made the transaction. Just the role for a computer!

To be fair I should record that an experienced box office clerk could tell a lot about the state of business from looking through the plans and assessing how full the books of tickets in the racks which lined every inch of wall space looked. The clerk could also ensure that ticket sales were so distributed that even a 'thin' audience would give a reasonable impression to those on stage. Another skill was the ability to turn over a pile of plans to find just the 3 seats the customer wanted – before the customer changed their mind. Let's face it, these weren't great days of customer care.

After a period of tackling the post I progressed to doing the 'advance'. For this activity I was found a desk in the manager's office in the afternoon while he was absent where I could sort out and count all the flimsy ticket stubs which had been sold that day. It seems unbelievable now that the whole sales accounting process could be done in this way. I am afraid this was not an activity I warmed to and was therefore given the task infrequently. It did, however, convince me of the need for a better way.

My box office mentor also enabled me to see a number of shows in other theatres. This was a matter of 'passing in': his term to describe arranging with a box office where there wasn't capacity business for me to go along and been shown to a seat by the manager without a ticket appearing anywhere along the line! That I have no particular memories of the shows I saw underlines, I think, that I wasn't harming sales; more memorable offerings had their tickets strictly controlled.

Whilst my working week was regularly Monday to Friday I found the Christmas schedule required my presence on Boxing Day so I braved the railway journey from Bath at an early hour with the Christmas leftovers to see me through the next few days. The Big Freeze of 1963 followed very quickly. As the country struggled to keep travelling and Aldwych theatregoers to claim their precious tickets for *King Lear* or *Comedy of Errors,* I desperately tried to keep warm, which in the Ladies meant sitting dangerously close to an ancient electric fire. It was probably this which speeded my interest in moving on to pastures new.

. . . .

Opera management - Rosebery Avenue

An advertisement in *The Stage* for an Assistant Manager at Sadler's Wells Theatre caught my attention in early January 1963. Whilst I had scant knowledge of the world of opera (amateur G&S in Bath, Frank Hauser's production of *Iolanthe* after the end of G&S copyright and a performance of *Pearl Fishers* at Sadler's Wells) I reckoned the Oxford management experience should stand me in good stead – and what about that vital box office experience which had been urged on me?

Much to my surprise the interview went well and a job offer followed. It would be wrong to say that the job description provided was a model of clarity; my new boss, Douglas Bailey, was an émigré from the commercial theatre where his many roles had included stage management for the Crazy Gang at the Victoria Palace. I am sure my Oxford background was significant to Duggie (as he was usually addressed) particularly as there were several other graduates around and he liked the idea of having someone to balance his commercial view. Opera planning was in the hands of Cambridge graduate Peter Hemmings who provided me with useful company background (and was later to mastermind the establishment of Scottish Opera).

In my first office. The carnation was part of the official dress code!

My news that I was leaving gave rise to a definite frostiness in the Aldwych box office. I think my career move to theatre management after barely six months was seen as a 'desertion' and Bill Shene's parting comment was a hope that I 'knew what I was doing'.

At the Wells, Duggie was very generous with his time explaining his take on theatre management. At the Aldwych the theatre manager still operated a morning and evening shift: checking the building was clean and tidy and doing the banking in the morning, and making sure the building front of house worked satisfactorily as far as the public were concerned in the evening (and at matinees). Whilst the Aldwych was the base for a regular group of RSC actors, at the Wells there were all parts of an opera company (principals, chorus, orchestra, dancers besides admin staff) to be looked after so the manager's role certainly didn't stop in the afternoon. Building maintenance, public and staff catering, and supervising what went on in the box office and how the booking leaflets were printed were all parts of the manager's responsibilities. Duggie made it seem that the place would fall apart if he wasn't there. It was certainly a different way of operation to the Aldwych.

I was thrown in at the deep end – I think the learning procedure was known as 'sitting by Nellie'; you basically watched what someone did and then had to do it whether the procedure was good or bad - I suspect mostly bad, these were not the days of detailed job procedures! The most challenging part of my new job was getting to grips with the world of catering, much to the amusement of my parents since I was not known for my prowess in the kitchen (still the case, except for my relationship with the dishwasher).

At the Wells catering was all-important and meant providing food and drink services both for the public and for everyone who worked in the building. With an opera company that was a lot of people - especially challenging as the facilities at the old Wells were limited. The crucial player in the catering function was the cook whose efforts either kept the company happy or brought about revolution. During my time this role was (amply) filled by a German lady with limited English but who managed to keep the peace most of the time as long as I got provisions delivered from her suppliers in Soho on time and I answered any complaints. Front of house catering had originally been a bar service with sandwiches but after a spell of complaints the Administrative Director, Stephen Arlen, had decreed there had to be change. Theatre catering (then as now) could either be undertaken by a separate organisation or provided in-house. Stephen wanted catering to be part of the total theatre experience – an expression I was to hear from him myself in later days and in line with Olivier's comments on one occasion to theatre attendants that how they greeted the audience affected how they viewed his performance.

As a result of Stephen's diktat an in-house catering operation had been established at the Wells and when I arrived I found an extensive buffet service as well as various bars in operation for the full hour before curtain up. To an extent this arrangement was part of getting the audience out to Islington since it was very much felt to be off the theatreland map. Although nearby Camden Passage had two well-known restaurants (Carrier's was one) the area had not as yet acquired its celebrity status. Indeed 'passing trade' rarely supported ticket sales – as I recall, the only production to generate a queue was Brecht/Weill's *The Rise and Fall of the City of Mahoganny*.

My instruction in dealing with the public at a performance was a matter of following Duggie as he 'walked the house' greeting regulars and raising an eyebrow if any of his staff seemed to be contravening his perception of their duties. Though any form of written job description was lacking there was considerable attention given to how the audience was treated and how the catering operated.

The only form of communication around the building was the house telephone so giving the clearance for a performance to begin entailed telephoning the stage manager in the prompt corner. When I was first left in sole charge for an evening by Duggie and had the responsibility of starting the performance I felt a great sense of achievement, though Duggie did ring from home to check all was ok! I am not sure Duggie ever came to grips with opera but I learnt a great deal from him – how to listen to comments, when to exhort staff, when to engage with the audience and when to be non-committal – all of which is nowadays the content of books, extensive courses and seminars.

During my time at the Wells we had some special performances which provided useful and amusing experience. At the planning session with the (female) organisers of one gala performance I was amazed at how much discussion there was about committee tickets. It wasn't the view of the stage that mattered, it seemed, but proximity to Princess Margaret who was the royal adding to the sense of occasion (and justifying the increased ticket prices)! On the occasion itself the line-up in the theatre foyer of those to be presented was carefully checked by Duggie against his detailed order of proceedings - but somehow a stranger got included and gave Duggie (and me) palpitations when he moved forward as if to kiss the Royal. 'Check and check again when dealing with VIP visitors' was a lesson learnt!

I had limited contact with Norman Tucker, the organisation's overall director, but on one occasion whilst on duty I had to explain to a member of the audience complaining that the person standing at the back of the Dress Circle rattling coins in his pocket was in fact the Director himself. My contact with other members of staff ranged from strictly business (canteen food, complimentary tickets!) to extensive conversations in a bar during the performance while waiting for an interval. On one or two occasions Tucker joined the staff who gathered in the Circle Bar during an act or after an interval and I picked up aa little more about the man who had been a senior administrator in the Treasury. During WWII and was obviously an extremely talented pianist. The latter accomplishment was often apparent when one passed his office and heard him playing.

These encounters provided me with a wealth of knowledge about the opera world and how it had developed. Warwick Braithwaite (a conductor who had originally been with the Carl Rosa Opera Company) and Peter Hemmings (opera planning) were generous of their time answering my searching questions and Edward Renton (whose assistant I would later become at the Coliseum) brought many stories of his time also with Carl Rosa. I knew nothing of this organisation which had never, as far as I was aware, made it to Bath. (They did to Bristol and I have a poster to prove it!) The drama of how the Arts Council had tried to solve the challenge of providing opera throughout the UK when Carl Rosa was on its last legs under the Phillips family filled in many an evening in the Circle Bar between intervals.

I also heard how in 1957 the Arts Council nearly effected the demise of Sadler's Wells with its proposal for amalgamation with Covent Garden and then Carl Rosa. Both plans were scuppered by the threatened resignations of the company's senior managers – Tucker, Arlen and Alex Gibson (the Music Director).A similar proposal to merge the Royal Opera House with the Wells - by then, English National Opera - was to emerge from the Arts Council some forty years later to similar howls of outrage.

Gradually the history of touring opera in the UK became a little clearer to me and I began to realise the significant part

Sadler's Wells Opera now played in the country's musical life. I learnt how the two separate parts of the company – known as Sadler's and Wells - took turns to tour productions, one company being on the road whilst the other was performing at the Rosebery Avenue base. Apparently the companies had originally been known as 'A' and 'B' until protests were received from some venues about being visited by the 'second' company. What a crush there was when both were briefly together in Rosebery Avenue before the company which had been in London went on the road with its repertoire. My greatest informant was Peter Hemmings, who was involved with a number of projects outside Sadler's Wells, most notably the New Opera Company . Both gave occasional small scale performances though their work did not greatly appeal to me. What did intrigue me were Peter's ideas for a separate opera company to tour Scotland…

Another informant was the Finance Officer, Russell Brown. He too was involved in a small scale company (Rostrum) which gave occasional performances. Russell left for Stratford during my time (to control, he said, Peter Hall's expenditure) but we kept in touch from then on. Russell was always a customer for a guest ticket however dire the show and good for arts gossip when we lunched together. He masterminded various exhibitions and mini festivals while at the Royal College of Art, (which he moved on to after Stratford): that on Prince Albert stays in my memory. Russell wasn't exactly a matinee idol as far as looks were concerned but always had a very attractive companion.

None of the opera background I acquired from these contacts was known to me before that day I arrived in early 1963 and I made a mental note for the future to give any staff I ever employed some idea of the history of the organisation they were joining.

Whilst at the Wells I had some contact with the Royal Opera House. There was an arrangement whereby chorus members could attend each other's dress rehearsals and making such Royal Opera House bookings were my responsibility. In many ways we were very much the poor relation; it was felt by many in the organisation that the Royal Opera House had hijacked both our ballet companies. It was of course the Sadler's Wells Ballet company that had given the first performance at Covent Garden when it reopened after the war. The company which remained at Rosebery Avenue, Sadler's Wells Theatre Ballet, also moved to the Opera House in 1955 leaving the Wells without a regular ballet company, though bus conductors still yelled "Sadler's Wells for opera and ballet" when the buses pulled up outside in my time! There was apparently little cooperation between the two organisations - on one occasion the Royal Opera House scheduled the same opera as Sadler's Wells! Nevertheless, Duggie felt he should follow the sartorial practice of ROH management and each first night swapped his normal dinner jacket for white tie and tails – much to the quiet amusement of his colleagues.

One of the tasks I was given and which led to a long term friendship was that of arranging the displays on the walls of the Circle Bar. I was told to 'ring up those chaps Mander and Mitchenson and get what you can' relating to the next production to enter the repertoire, *La Belle Hélène*. The telephone call was duly made and I had an experience which was to be repeated many times over the years of joining a conversation/argument between Ray and Joe on two telephones in different parts of their house about what they might be able to let us have. I soon realised why Noel Coward called them Gog and Magog without identifying who was who. They kept on talking about someone called Boo and it took some while for me to realise they were talking about Evelyn Laye, who was known by that name by many of her friends. Items were duly hand-delivered when Ray and Joe next came to a show (they were the Wells' official archivists so had regular comps – on one visit they brought the young Judi Dench who had just taken on one of their kittens). I would set about making up a display with what had been delivered – which often meant a fair amount of restoration. Ray and Joe had incredible material but there was rather a lot of Sellotape used until later years saw guidance from NADFAS volunteers.

Sadler's Wells was a mix of family home and artistic factory. There was always camaraderie in the canteen but there was rarely a space in the building which wasn't being used by company members in some way. This made getting about the building something of a challenge but established lots of nodding acquaintances as I mouthed apologies to members of the music staff taking sessions in a bar as

I passed through; I didn't need to be told we were short of space! As months passed I became aware of references (in *The Stage*, of course) to the establishment, at last, of a National Theatre and also perhaps a new home to replace the cramped conditions at Rosebery Avenue. As the summer of '63 progressed and the Wells played host to Rambert Ballet I registered that our admin boss, Stephen Arlen, had been appointed as the National's administrative director to work alongside Laurence Olivier who had been appointed Director earlier. We all realised that Stephen Arlen now had an even busier schedule.

None of this impacted on my routine until one day Duggie told me in a rather serious voice that the 'boss' (as he always referred to Arlen) wanted to see me. Wondering what I had done or failed to do I duly presented myself and was told to 'park my bum and listen'. I was then asked after minimal preliminaries if I would like to go and be the manager at the Old Vic which was in the course of being set up as the temporary home of the new National Theatre. I cannot be sure how I responded but I certainly didn't refuse and it was agreed that there would be a further meeting very soon.

Duggie was already aware of what was being offered (implying much recommendation from him) and made it quite clear I could rely on his support if I went. There wasn't really any doubt in my mind so a further meeting saw me saying 'yes please'.

For the record I should mention here that the person who had initially been selected as manager after responding to an advertisement and interview had withdrawn because of family illness. My own experience with Stephen Arlen over this appointment and seeing him in action later made me aware that he had his own way of doing things which didn't necessarily fit standard practice but got results.

EARLY DAYS IN THE WATERLOO ROAD

The National Theatre at the Old Vic

I started my career with the National Theatre in the August before the first performance in October 1963. My first visit to the Old Vic - and very first meeting with 'Sir' (the National's director, Laurence Olivier) saw the place full of activity - everywhere one went there were workmen. I had made one or two trips to Old Vic productions whilst at school but I wasn't at all familiar with the building so going round with Stephen Arlen and hearing about such and such wall coming down didn't mean much other than there was a lot of work ahead. To some the National was behaving outrageously in removing the flock wallpaper and cosy corners. There was no grand plan as such (certainly no theatre consultant) other than to create a different atmosphere. The Sean Kenny stage alterations with a new revolve and removal of stage boxes was in full swing. There was an architectural practice involved, Fred Rowntree and Co., but the representative I met, Martin Card, was clearly in thrall to Olivier, Arlen and Co. Stephen was much concerned with opening up spaces front of house and using bright coloured hessian wall hangings certainly created a different atmosphere: gilt remained around the circle fronts but elsewhere the auditorium was what became known as sludge green. The front 6 rows of the gallery were reseated and given individual seats so as to create an Upper Circle of 3 rows. The dress circle was also reseated but for various reasons with poor sight lines – giving rise to later complaints, notably from one patron with the memorable question to me about the discomfort experienced: "My wife's pregnant - what are you going to do about it?" Collapse all round.

*The celebrated huts in Aquinas Street which housed the offices
and rehearsal room for the NT until the move to the South Bank*

*The Archway, 10A Aquinas Street in 2013 showing
the housing which replaced the NT offices*

In order to create much needed space both front and rear of house and enable the Old Vic to work in its new role, the senior administration was housed in a series of wooden huts provided by the builders McAlpine. These were located on a former bomb site made available by the GLC a short distance away from the theatre. Initially with the address of 22 Duchy Street but then changed to a more intriguing and geographically correct 'The Archway', 10a Aquinas Street, these huts were the base for some of the National's momentous early decisions. As time passed more huts were squeezed onto the site so that it eventually provided a boardroom and rehearsal rooms besides a myriad of offices. The office used by Olivier was eventually soundproofed when it was found that visitors waiting in the entrance lobby could enjoy his distinctive voice delivering some of his rather confidential opinions! The atmosphere at these offices sometimes seemed a world apart from that at the theatre only fifteen minutes' brisk walk away. I became responsible for 'servicing' them – catering, housekeeping, security – which was often a challenge, sometimes an embarrassment: I recall being tracked down in the small hours when the alarm system was activated, which could have been by stray cats or strong winds such was the flimsy structure that was the National's administrative base.

When I paid a nostalgic trip to Waterloo around the fiftieth anniversary of the National's first performance I was amazed to see how the site (including its valuable car parking spaces) had been transformed into obviously very desirable homes within walking distance of all that the South Bank had to offer!

The success of the Old Vic Company's presentation of all of Shakespeare's first folio in the 1950s had funded the building of an annexe across the road from the Vic in Webber Street. This housed a paint frame, making wardrobe and large carpenters' workshop so the National had the luxury of such important technical facilities close at hand when it got under way. Again this was an area where responsibility for housekeeping came my way. Over the years I found myself in a love/hate relationship with one resident of this building – Ivan Alderman. As his obituary recorded he was "the most eccentric and talented costume supervisor to dress actors and actresses" Ivan almost made the Annexe his home as he kept very strange hours so was a nightmare as far as security was concerned. I am not sure he ever went home! But the results of his labours on stage were certainly magnificent and made one forget our spats about cleaning and hygiene.

Many other theatre craft technicians continued on from the Old Vic Company to the new National organisation and many knew Olivier from his 1930s time with the company. The armourer, Reg Amos, had joined when a boy and stayed until retirement. Similarly the head of the carpenters' workshop, Bill Parker - a real craftsman (and strong union man). I am sure these very experienced colleagues must have smiled quietly at my youthful enthusiasm.

One long serving employee, Harry Henderson, became invaluable. Harry ('arry) was a traditional South

Londoner and could fix most things either himself (he was a regular weightlifter who always managed to find space for his weights somewhere in the building) or through his extended family (both his brothers were recruited by me, one for security and another for maintenance, as was his wife, Adrienne, who later did part time work in the box office – she had worked at the Streatham Hill theatre in its pre-bingo hall days). Harry had supervised all cleaning in the daytime before donning commissionaire's garb in the evening in Old Vic days. He was a character who made sure he was in the right place at the right time. He swiftly signed up to the National when it arrived and identified me as the boss to follow. Perhaps this was as a result of his army career (India and Egypt, where he was badly injured and nearly lost his arm) and knowing who to report to! We established excellent relations, particularly after I replaced his commissionaire's uniform with a black coat and striped trousers (echoing a bank clerk in those days) for evening front of house duties. Harry wasn't the easiest person to work with and on many an occasion I had to make peace between Harry and someone he thought had been shirking – even if it was not his department. We had as house carpenter a splendid Italian (I think), Frank Fresko, who came to the Vic after retirement from Bristol Old Vic. Each week there seemed to be an issue between him and Harry to sort out! Of course, after I left Harry served the next boss with similar devotion! The Vicar of Bray springs to mind.

Ernie Davis, stage door keeper extraordinaire

In the summer of 1963 days and weeks rushed by and somehow I got my head round equipping the catering areas and recruiting new theatre staff to check tickets, sell programmes and operate bars and buffets which were to follow the Sadler's Wells example. One or two members of the Old Vic company era signed up to work for the National but as there was a desire to create a new atmosphere I aimed to find new blood that I could get to follow my aims. I don't recall any particular briefing from Arlen on this but attendance at occasional planning meetings and general conversation made it clear that the National wanted to offer a different atmosphere to its public. Even so, we assembled a real family of bar and buffet staff, and traditional theatre 'characters' like the wonderful Ernie Davis at the Stage Door. Ernie was the epitome of a stage door keeper, knowing every artist (and their other halves), when converse should be brief and when not, how to marshal autograph hunters so they went away satisfied, and above all when to say no to callers.

. . . .

Early challenges

Whilst setting up the catering meant starting from scratch, the booking arrangements were already in the hands of an old-school box office manager, Pat Layton. He had worked for the great theatrical family of the Alberys at the New Theatre in St Martin's Lane and had therefore been on the spot across the road from the National's first offices in Goodwin's Court to badger the Board Secretary, Kenneth Rae, for a job when the go-ahead was given for the National to start at the Old Vic as its temporary home. Pat was already in post when I arrived and before booking opened for the first performances we had little time for much contact. When booking did open and the sacks of mail arrived with each post, Pat was frequently at my office door reporting that he had never seen so much mail.

I suppose it was inevitable that after over 100 years talking about a National Theatre its actual arrival should provoke a lot of interest, but as time passed it became clear the demand for tickets was not just a passing interest. The productions in the National's first months included twenty two performances of *Hamlet*, directed by Olivier (with Peter O'Toole fresh from filming Lawrence of Arabia, as the Prince of Denmark) and while other productions were to be continued in the repertoire it was known that *Hamlet* would not. Cue for major flood of angry patrons' letters unable to get tickets; it was here that Pat made it clear that such correspondence was my responsibility! I came up with a detailed explanation of limited seating capacity/finite number of performances/unprecedented public demand and employed a secretary to type a large number of replies. I even got one or two letters back thanking me for a 'full explanation'.

The first performance ever by the National Theatre was on October 22 1963 – it was apparently originally scheduled for the day before but the Chairman, Lord Chandos, had insisted it be changed from Trafalgar Day. I could never understand this insistence – wasn't Trafalgar a great British triumph anyway? There was no particular pomp associated with the occasion. There had been much discussion over who got tickets – many of the names who were awarded the distinction of attendance didn't mean much to me at the time but their role in the battle for the company later emerged. One personality I did recognise amongst the throng that night was Selwyn Lloyd who had been Chancellor when Parliament had given the go ahead for the National. The post-performance celebration, in the scruffy rehearsal room backstage at the Old Vic, was a nightmare to organise but it was made for me by Olivier complimenting my organising skills whilst introducing me to Chichester's Pieter Rogers, who understandably didn't recall our first encounter. It was also, I think, the first occasion I was called 'Rupie' – Sir delighted in using his own version of one's first name, a mark of being recognised as special in some way. I was always 'Rupie' from then on.

St Joan (with a wonderful portrayal of the Maid by Joan Plowright) followed on from *Hamlet* and then there was *Uncle Vanya* (like *St Joan* transferred from Chichester as Olivier based his first ensemble on that he had assembled there), with *The Recruiting Officer* before Christmas. *Hamlet* had not enjoyed particularly good notices (but then every performance was already sold out before it opened) and the new stage revolve was a constant source of trouble – often requiring manual labour to move from whoever happened to be available, but there was a general feeling that everything was on a roll and the company was a SUCCESS. This continued with *Hobson's Choice* but Max Frisch's *Andorra* and certainly the double bill of Beckett's *Play* coupled with Sophocles' *Philoctetes* early in 1964 saw some empty seats for the first time. The cast list for *Andorra* even included a simple questionnaire to glean audience views. I always thought this was the Royal Court influence at work. It was directed by Lindsay Anderson and our associate directors John Dexter and Bill Gaskill who came to the National from Sloane Square, as did the delightful Sunny Amey who was Sir's PA. I am not sure anything came from the questionnaire exercise! *Andorra* had a catchy piece of music by Ron Grainer (recorded by UK guitar band The Eagles), EP records of which I arranged to be sold by our usherettes; the interest was a spur to investigate a bookstall.

We got back to overflowing houses with *Othello* (the Shakespeare quatercentenary offering) and, initially, *The Master Builder* with Michael Redgrave. Public support at the box office challenged both the ability of the box office to cope and made the planning department uncertain of the number of performances to schedule.

The National, like the Old Vic previously and in line with most other subsidised companies at the time, relied on members of the public joining for a nominal fee a mailing list to receive advance information. Initially the National gave its mailing list members an advance booking date so they could get in their requests before the general public. All fine if requests could be dealt with before the general date - but if not? And what if the leaflet failed to arrive in the post? We had these challenges in abundance. However many people we employed in the box office we struggled to process those early bookings fast enough; even more of a problem was the stream of complaints we received about not getting publicity. Our mailing operation relied on a machine which printed names and addresses from a stencil on a card surround. We found (after some very lengthy late night sessions) that unfortunately our elderly machine missed certain addresses so those poor people never got their leaflets and didn't therefore stand any chance to book tickets! These experiences led to major rethinking of how we should handle this crucial area.

The first attempt to sort out the problem involved some management consultants who provided, after lengthy sessions with myself and box office personnel, some conclusions which were of no great help: "put on more performances of popular productions, increase prices to reduce demand." Not exactly earth shattering and not appropriate for a subsidised theatre company. In a meeting with Stephen Arlen I remember complaining that a lot of what had been written by the consultants about our problem was simply a regurgitation of what they had been told by me. "Makes one do a lot of thinking" was his response and that was what we did for many long days and evenings.

The solution we came up with to the mailing problem was drastic but effective. Instead of relying on an addressing machine (it would be many years before computers took over this task – we didn't even have calculators!) we made it the responsibility of the patron to signify their wish to receive information by giving them a card which they addressed to themselves and sent us so that it could be used in a window envelope to mail out the publicity leaflet. Not rocket technology, but since the mailing process now simply amounted to filling envelopes this meant we could offer a free service with the onus on the patron to get their address card to us.

The consultants' report had made various suggestions about subscription schemes which had us investigating the subscription voucher scheme then used by the Royal Opera House but we concluded it would give a bad impression (certainly not in line with being a National Theatre for all!) and not really help. The consultants had found that our patrons tended to book regularly for the same ticket prices so we decided to ask patrons to restrict their booking to a single price category. These were divided into top prices (A), middle prices (B) and cheapest prices (C) so that if different envelopes were used the booking mail could be sorted by temporary staff according to price category wanted. The pack the patron received contained specially marked labels (A, B or C according to ticket price) to ease sorting at the theatre.

When Arlen saw one of these he fired off a typical note:

"My God! All that paper that suddenly arrived. I have managed to stick A on week beginning 19th September and B over 1 on page 1, C I can find no place for. The question is, do I get any tickets, or, if I stick C on the form and C on the front of my car, would you provide me with parking facilities?"

With a postscript:

"Nobody could say you don't try!"

The Old Vic (like the Aldwych) had a very small box office so we made the case for a larger space which could be handed over to separate staff to concentrate solely on the advance bookings for a dedicated period. Fortunately, we could squeeze in yet another hut at Aquinas Street. Gradually we managed to process our patrons' postal requests before we got to open the booking in person at the box office itself.

All of this brought screams not only from the public ("My God, all that paper!") but also from colleagues – leaflets had to be prepared and sent out to allow sufficient time for the booking operation and this meant programming decisions couldn't be made at the last minute: "Why is this front of house chap sending notes around telling us to make rep decisions so far ahead?" Eventually the message got across!

There were some simple steps taken to help those intrepid individuals who came to the Waterloo Road to book in person, although Pat (like my boss at the Aldwych) believed a long visible queue was always a good advertisement. We produced a large board giving details of ticket availability for each date of a production which became known as the 'noughts and crosses board'. On one occasion Olivier, viewing the blanks indicating considerable availability for *The Master Builder* in which he had succeeded Redgrave as Solness, remarked "If they won't come, I won't do it". Simple supply and demand, leading to mid-week *Othello* matinees being scheduled to replace the less popular *Master Builder*.

At the box office itself we also brought about some revolutionary changes. Traditionally, the clerk selling tickets sat behind a closed window/screen interacting with the customer through a small square opening - the reasoning being that not only was the cash inside protected, but also the information on the all-important plans. Eventually Pat was persuaded that, even if the patron could see what was on the plan, they would be extremely unlikely to understand what all the scribbles meant. Further, by removing the screen, a more natural conversation including body language could take place. The customer might even then believe it when told a performance was sold out! Pat was also persuaded to accept identification of staff by the use of short boards bearing their names displayed to the patron at the box office window. The final triumph was Pat's acceptance of diagrams clearly showing price divisions. Pat was lucky with his team – some traditional and some forward thinking. For a time Simon Callow was on the staff, his letter begging to do 'something' was passed to me and from me to Pat to fill a vacancy in the box office front line. Simon gives a more embroidered account of his employment in his account of the National's early years, describing the front of house operation as "strictly disciplined" under my "almost military leadership". I think this was a compliment…

Another employee, until we fell out over my refusal to give a £1 per week salary increase, was Roger Lobb who later returned to the National, masterminding the whole box office operation on the South Bank, as well as being the driving force behind the international box office managers' organisation (SOBOM). He became a good friend of ours despite that missing pound.

*One of the special desks set up in the Old Vic foyer
for the first day of a new booking period, seen
here in a posed shot with staff members!*

Perhaps my most revolutionary change to the box office
was the arrangement brought in on the first day of booking
for a fresh run of performances. My assistant and I decided
that a new approach was needed so instead of having patrons
wait in line outside the building they were invited in and
given coffee having registered their place in the queue with
a numbered ticket from a dispenser. They were then invited
to the foyer in small groups where tables with plans for the
productions on offer were arranged. Once the patron had
made the rounds of the tables they went to the box office
window itself where tickets were issued against the slip on
which the various bookings had been recorded. Even if all

this took time the patron hadn't been standing in line for an extended period. There were some who when faced with our 'place-in-the-queue' ticket machine protested "But I <u>want</u> to stand and queue!"

Our open plan customer-friendly box office

I felt the changes we brought about in booking arrangements were certainly worth the long hours of analysis and persuasion involved. Not so many years later computers would consign almost all of these arrangements to history and most of the time (!) keep the customer happy. For me, these experiences dealing with the National's early demands were invaluable when discussing booking systems with the computer whizz kids who came on the scene as the years passed. Although I had many discussions with computer firms both at the Old Vic and later at the Coliseum I never actually installed a system and it was in my time with SOLT/TMA that the last traditional paper tickets (in three sections, torn from a book of tickets) in the West End passed into oblivion. They were from the Fortune Theatre run by Paul Gane who donated a set to the Mander & Mitchenson Collection.

Whilst I felt reasonably at ease transforming the booking operation (some said making everything so complicated, of course) I found it more of a challenge to achieve something special as far as catering was concerned. Staff catering was a particular challenge. Not only were the surroundings cramped backstage at the Old Vic, but actors wanted more substantial meals available for longer hours than I had been used to with singers. There was also the challenge of providing similar at Aquinas Street. For many years the operation there was brilliantly provided by a homely Italian lady, Anna, who lived nearby. Her successor, Rose, was even more of a character who provided some memorable menu items, 'sooty' potatoes being the best. Public catering at the Vic followed the pattern of cold buffets as at Sadler's Wells and with wonderful local staff running the buffets and mostly young barmen we gradually found we kept patrons happy. I had been able to persuade Stephen Arlen after a few months of the National's public operation that I needed an assistant (recruiting a wonderful character, James – Jimmy - Walters) but making more sense of catering was down to me.

My early recruits as catering supervisor were not successful but eventually I was able to find someone who wanted to move on from catering for West End theatre managements. Chris Simpson brought a wealth of stories from his past (for example, how to eke out an extra portion from each catering tub of ice cream in order to make a little extra income for the server) and accepted the challenge of making the National's catering noteworthy for audiences and at least acceptable for staff. Chris was an early champion of microwave cooking. Unfortunately, microwaves were still in their early development and my stomach suffered a great deal from microwaved meals taken in the cause of research. Somehow the dress circle bar took on the role of a mini restaurant with pre-booked tables and table service. The kitchen arrangements downstairs in the basement were not ones I care to remember in detail but the South African 'chef' Ruby was certainly competent in producing the various sandwiches and platters we offered two floors up. Looking back I think the catering operation was a great achievement given the limited surroundings. This was largely due to Chris (who probably had his own arrangements with suppliers) but he was always striving to do more. It was Chris who first introduced me to job descriptions and staff handbooks, but I think beyond that it was the overall atmosphere of the organisation that got the best out of staff – not just in the catering operation.

· ·

Ranged left

The sixties brought a new approach to theatre print design, as it did in many spheres of business at this time most noticeably banking and insurance. Stephen Arlen had already taken some steps to change the image of Sadler's Wells at Rosebery Avenue with bold modern typography on the leaflets giving performance details (even if the nightly programmes were of a previous vintage) so he was obviously anxious for the new National Theatre to project a particular image. In this respect Ken Tynan, who had been appointed Literary Manager at an early stage, was an ideal collaborator.

I had been vaguely aware during my time at Sadler's Wells of the involvement of a graphic designer in setting out all the information on a leaflet and in early days at the National sat in on Arlen's meetings with the character who had been given the responsibility of portraying the National Theatre in print: Ken Briggs. Ken had trained at Central School and was a brilliant exponent of modern typography, which my assistant Jimmy and I always cheekily referred to as 'ranged left'. The National's very first red and black leaflet was a great example of this modern design but brought howls from traditionalists, especially those who had been devotees of the Old Vic Company's yellow and black booklet. At this stage my role was very much limited to observation and it was only later that I drove Ken mad by requiring booking forms and associated information sheets to be designed. However early we started on collating information from the planning departments, it never seemed there was enough time for Ken to have it laid out for the printer so the target delivery date could be kept. Fortunately we also had a very good printer for this work: Maurice Jackson whose firm King & Jackson had been long associated with theatre print. Maurice (married to a former variety artist) was a fund of stories about the theatre world – and always good at getting the job done on time.

As Literary Manager, programmes were very much Ken Tynan's responsibility (as were all PR matters but that merits separate comment). Ken always vetted the editorial content of leaflets but his particular speciality was the creation of the National's programmes which were intended to provide interesting information about the play, its interpretation if necessary, and any contemporary background. A complete contrast to West End programmes of the period which were, as he put it, 'cast lists surrounded by gin adverts'. At the National, cast details were given in a free cast list, entirely separate from programmes which could be purchased. This arrangement took some getting over to the front of house staff (we could call them usherettes in those days) who found it hard to *give away* essential information and had to be reminded at every performance that, whilst the programmes cost 1'/6" [17.5p], the cast lists were absolutely free. Although the RSC made cast sheets freely available at Stratford, this was not the case at their London base, the Aldwych, because of contractual arrangements.

The new-style programmes, initially without any adverts, earned a lot of plaudits for the National but as time went by there were many discussions at board level about the costs involved (and one or two about design when the typography challenged those with less than perfect sight!). The chairman, Lord Chandos, did at one stage consider an arrangement for the publishers of the American free theatre programme, *Playbill*, to take over and relieve the National of all financial responsibility – or so the story filtered down to us – but the programmes continued to earn us many compliments and sell well which of course meant there were regular in-house suggestions that we raise their price.

Responsibility for ensuring that there were sufficient programmes available each performance fell to me so it was a matter of judging how likely a particular production's audience were to buy a programme. Whilst the free cast lists featured in a publicity budget if I ordered a programme quantity which resulted in a large number being unsold it was laid at my door as overordering. Gradually I acquired an ability to decide if programme demand was likely to be 'one between two' or more thinly spread, and formed a productive working relationship with another print firm, headed by someone of my age, which took pride in helping to get things right – and still make a profit. The company with a dedicated and knowledgeable staff, Battley Brothers, remained as programme printers to the National until they amalgamated with another firm many years later. Their MD, Bernard Battley, remained a close contact for all my time in theatre management.

*Ken Brigg's poster for the inaugural National Theatre
production (image courtesy of the National Theatre Archive)*

Another aspect of publicity which came my way was the National's posters. Just as the leaflets with performance details conveyed a modern image so too did the posters. I first became aware of that for *Hamlet* when copies arrived and I had to get them billposted around the Old Vic in double quick time. The large (quad crown) poster featured a tiny Peter O'Toole on a white strip across a black background with the title, *Hamlet*, cast and performance details in red. It was quickly dubbed, rather aptly I thought, 'cinemascope'. For the first season there were striking visual posters which attracted a lot of favourable comment but there was always a battle to get them printed and billposted in time. Although Ken (Briggs, difficult having two Kens involved in same area!) was never one to be ahead of time, to be fair he had quite a battle extracting production details from the artistic team.

As well as ensuring that posters were up at the theatre for the first night I also had to have them covered up in some way after the last performance – or risk a message from 'Sir' about the bills not being blanked out. A reminder of the actor manager! The attention he could give to such matters (comparing the colour of one season's leaflets with the previous and sending a postcard to Sue because of its colour while on a Canadian tour - "a splendid blue, don't you think?" - and on another sending a cryptic message to Sunny Amey: "Keep Spring green for leaflets but use yellow for bills") was both amazing and infuriating to us lesser mortals. Arlen likened it to Olivier's way of relaxing, much as others might go to the cinema. Some commentators spoke admiringly of how Olivier was involved in these day-to-day details, implying there was no administrator around whose actual job it was to do these things. To myself and colleagues Olivier could indeed be bewilderingly into the minute detail - maddeningly, he would pass messages about posters needing to change via the fireman when leaving the theatre after a show. (Back in the day every theatre had an on-site fireman – usually an ex-regular firefighter – to oversee fire safety and security when the theatre was closed.) For all these sometimes trying interventions, there was certainly a close working relationship with Arlen as Administrative Director in those early National years - as

Olivier's emotional performance after Arlen's death at a memorial performance in 1972 testified.

As the large quad crown full colour posters were rarely used beyond the Old Vic their expense brought about their replacement with large black and white photographs which made a striking display down the Waterloo Road. There was a marvellous image of Olivier as Othello holding a rose which I made sure I rescued from the salvage pile and remained in our possession until it passed to the Olivier family archives (obviously secreted given its un-PC nature with Olivier blacked up!). The National used a variety of photographers for production shots including Snowdon and Angus McBean. The latter still used a plate camera prompting 'Sir' to remark one day when he saw McBean in action with tripod and hood, 'how much photography has advanced in the last 100 years'.

When the National was forced by poor business to take advertising spaces on hoardings and on London Transport sites, smaller (double crown) posters were produced. These were often the subject of requests from the public, as were the company's programmes. It was therefore a natural step to try and exploit this interest in some organised way rather than theatre management having to deal with requests as and when time permitted. The Old Vic barely had enough space to provide food and drink for audiences (even after removing a lot of walls) so it was quite a challenge to persuade the licensing authority to allow us to create a bookstand, (as opposed to a bookstall - a subtle distinction!) We did, eventually, in the corridor behind the stalls, and find 'resting' young dancers agile enough to make the space work. For many years we employed a splendid character to run this operation, Joan Panton. She worked for us and then went off to Churchills nightclub every evening – as a dresser.

Sadly, copies of those first posters are now something of a rarity as the original silk screen printers' premises were burnt down along with the stock they were storing. The file copies I religiously amassed at the Old Vic were mostly lost (deliberately destroyed?) in the move to the South Bank. I am not sure what the NT archive has been able to salvage nor what might exist at the V&A's theatre collection (assuming it is still identifiable).

Ken Briggs' influence eventually extended to designing more than publicity items. It wasn't a matter of being specifically commissioned to produce a house style (as was happening at the time with the banks and insurance companies), but of meeting requests such as 'could you do a layout for notepaper as we need some' or 'we think these slips should look more like everything else' with a unifying design approach. I took an interest in this activity as I certainly believed everything should look as if it belonged. I know I drove colleagues mad when I produced a guidance note of how to lay out a letter on the notepaper Ken designed. Inevitably this was a matter of ranging the text left and omitting unnecessary punctuation – there were those who delighted in doing the opposite! In the box office area I arranged a whole range of stationery, carefully colour-coded slips, to avoid staff having to write notes on generic compliment slips about 'cheque not signed' or some such issue. As Roger Lobb later revealed to me there was quite a competition amongst his colleagues to see what they could dream up which deliberately fell between the gaps in my precious colour-coded scheme... innocent fun.

Sue in the one easy chair in the Manager's Office

My involvement in these design matters was partly by chance, partly by initiative and partly because, as I was willing, it seemed a good idea to my boss to allow/encourage it! We – by this I mean myself and the two people who worked as my assistants (Jimmy Walters and then St John Sandringham) – also had a theory that a National Theatre would need matters such as stationery organised on a central basis. This bit of empire building was helped in its early days by our Finance Officer being more interested in ordering carbon paper and loo rolls than actually doing the sums. That's perhaps a little exaggeration, but when he left to go off to Canada his successor had a much better ability to explain budgets and results to departmental managers like myself, sometimes involving Lego blocks – the days before flip charts or PowerPoint presentations!

Gradually the belief that everything from print to signage at the theatre or on our vehicles should be in the same consistent style was adopted in all departments - but that added to the design workload and meant extended timescales. Solution: Ken was allowed to recruit an assistant to work as the in-house graphic designer. By now in this narrative my interest in design will have become clear; Ken's choice of Sue Chennells (who came from the commercial practice of Dewar Mills Associates) to fill the new appointment gave me an added reason for interest, and Sue and I found ourselves with a lot to discuss, not always work related.

Sue recalls our first meeting as an occasion when Jimmy and I exploded into her office having worked out how signage at the Vic should look. An incredible midnight performance with a galaxy of stars (Olivier - giving his Archie Rice, Sybil Thorndike, Lewis Casson, Alec Guinness, Joan Plowright, both Lynn and Vanessa Redgrave and many more) on June 13 1966 to mark the recent death of George Devine and celebrate his work at the Royal Court, required a special programme. Cast and other details changed constantly right up to the last moment so the finished programme only bore a slight resemblance to the performance itself and had needed much liaison with Sue to achieve anything which could be printed to our deadline. The liaison paid off and Battleys, as ever, managed to deliver something just in time. Sue and I relaxed after the performance to an unholy hour, this being the start of a wonderful relationship which has lasted more than half a century. Driving into the West End to check poster sites for the National's forthcoming season at the Queen's Theatre that summer, on the evening after England had won the World Cup, totally oblivious of the triumph as we had been working at the dark theatre on photo displays and wondering why everywhere was so crowded, did however nearly bring our relationship to an early end.

A major part of a theatre manager's job is obviously ensuring everything is in order for the safety and security of audience and performers. In the early months of the National's life I found this side of my job highly enjoyable but exhausting – it was some time before I could convince Arlen that I needed someone to share the performance duties and everything else. My choice fell on an individual who was working at Hampstead Theatre Club, was previously on the music staff at the Royal Opera House, and had studied music in Germany. This was Jimmy Walters, who has already been mentioned. A great character who was fun to work with and made a significant contribution to many parts of our work, being especially good at never accepting the simple answer but forever asking 'why?' Although conventional in attire while part of the management, after leaving the National Jimmy's sartorial dress became more way out (purple velvet suit and afro hair style). Once, when both of us had returned to the Vic for a public dress rehearsal, Sir said simply to him "You must have been very unhappy in a DJ". I was never sure of the detail but I believe Jimmy had been instrumental in presenting Gillian Lynne's dance review *'Collages'* at the Savoy Theatre early in 1963.

As theatre manager caught off duty

Given the National's popularity it was inevitable that the great and the good wanted seats so there was usually a VIP of some kind attending each performance. Very often there was a need to offer such visitors a drink in the interval on behalf of Sir, which was not an easy task in the crowded bars. Some needed more particular hospitality which necessitated negotiating the route to my office above the Dress Circle. All very well as long as I arranged for the performance not to continue until I had signalled to stage management that our VIP was safely returned to the auditorium. This was usually no problem but when *Othello* entered the repertoire and Sir was returning home to Brighton after a performance, every second counted. Diana Boddington, a formidable stage manager who had worked with Olivier on innumerable productions over the years and ran *Othello* performances, could be terrifying to defy. My most difficult encounter was when Constantine (still in post as the King of Greece) was scheduled to be using house seats for an *Othello* evening performance. He failed to arrive by 7.30 curtain up and the minutes ticked by. Eventually, faced with a tirade from Diana, I gave the go ahead for curtain up. Seconds later a Rolls screeched across the Waterloo Road to the front doors and I had no alternative but to escort HM to his seats, contrary to all our rules about not admitting latecomers. (The statement in our leaflets beginning 'Those who have the *misfortune* to arrive late...', was, we reckoned, a good example of our PR.) Many years later when Constantine, now ex-King of Greece, was collecting his tickets for a

Nureyev performance at the Coliseum box office and I was in the foyer I was almost tempted to remind him of our previous meeting!

We had a number of visits from Princess Margaret in a private capacity but Kenneth Rae, the Secretary of the Board (and scrupulous in observing correct social behaviour) as the theatre's licensee usually came to the theatre, greeted Margaret at the door and then handed over to me to conduct her to her seats and look after her for the rest of the evening. Over time this became almost second nature and routine. However, on one occasion Kenneth decided that his own dinner engagement must take priority and even though it was a party of six, told me that 'as you do it so well' he would leave everything to me. When the Rolls pulled up Margaret's husband, Snowdon, got out, stood to one side and was followed by a familiar looking tall blonde gentleman who stood aside in turn for Margaret who was then followed by her sister, the Queen. It turned out to be a family birthday outing to the theatre. On previous visits by Margaret I had encountered her detective and knew what was expected. Whenever the Queen came, however, her detective (Perkins) was very much more demanding. We had further private visits by the Queen and it became a little easier to anticipate the detective's rather peremptory demands for programmes and the clearing of gangways. On the occasion Mountbatten (Uncle Dickie) was in the Queen's party, I apparently acted incorrectly by asking if HM would sign the visitors' book I had by now purchased (from Asprey,

I think. Wonder who has that now?). Mountbatten made it clear that I shouldn't make such intrusive requests and should stick to pouring the drinks!

There was very little room in my office (shared during the day with my secretary – for many years a very efficient and attractive blonde called Elizabeth Taylor!) and only occasionally did I organise a member of the catering staff to be in attendance to pour drinks and circulate the sandwiches during interval entertaining. However daintily the sandwiches were prepared, Margaret always managed to leave something on her plate, inevitably with cigarette remains. Her mother, the Queen Mother, also managed the climb to my office for interval drinks and her visit coincided on one memorable occasion with that of Andrei Gromyko, at this time the Soviet Foreign Minister; their conversation via the interpreter apparently centred around horse racing matters! I think my favourite memory is of the Queen looking at a postcard of Sydney Opera House on my office notice board and wondering how much it was now going to cost before completion!

During my time at the Old Vic we had one 'formal' royal occasion: a performance of *As You Like It* on May 14, 1968. Perhaps it was the historian manque in me that had latched on to this particular date and set me persuading my superiors that it was something to celebrate. Initially no one was keen as there was a reluctance amongst National personnel to promote Old Vic history which I could not understand. Finally it was agreed that there should be "A special performance in celebration of the 150th anniversary of the opening of The Royal Coburg Theatre, now known as The Old Vic, in the presence of HRH The Princess Marina, Duchess of Kent".

The early days of my theatre post card collection, with not an official paper in sight on my office notice board!

Although I had gathered the essential facts about Lilian Baylis and her work at Sadler's Wells and The Old Vic whilst working at Sadler's Wells, it was conversations over many evenings that I learned from Yolande Bird the intricate history of the Vic and the origins of the National itself. As the assistant to the National's Board Secretary, Kenneth Rae, Yolande, who became a great family friend as years passed, was a fount of knowledge about the origins of the National: how after WWII the Old Vic organisation overcame their reservations to return to the theatre closed by bomb damage in 1941; how a grandly named Joint Council involving Stratford and Sadler's Wells as well as the Old Vic Company was established to plan for a National Theatre. I learnt much about the Old Vic Theatre Centre, established in 1946, and the personalities associated with it: Michel St Denis, Glen Byam Shaw and George Devine; how it operated from the patched-up theatre with the aim of being a "centre for training, research and experiment... a testing ground for new talent in all branches of theatre activity, opportunities for new ideas... methods of production". Also of the school established a year later under Glen Byam Shaw's direction which operated there until 1950; the new young company which took shows on tour as The Young Vic; the dismissal of Olivier as Director of the main company while heading a very successful tour of Australia and New Zealand in 1948; the move back from Bronson Albery's New Theatre in the West End to the restored Old Vic in November 1950, and the perennial disagreements between governors and directors with a major bust up in 1951 over, it seemed to me, who was really in control (pretty difficult given numbers involved I reckoned). Quite a history!

My head spun as Yolande recounted these events with which she had been so directly involved – as a student at the school, as business manager and public relations officer for The Young Vic and, after a spell with the Bristol Old Vic, as assistant to Kenneth Rae on the Joint Council planning for a National Theatre. Finally, she recounted how, after the Government and GLC voted funds, it was agreed that the Old Vic company should be disbanded in 1962 and a new company under Olivier take over the Old Vic as its temporary home. Not surprising really that there should be doubts about celebrating Old Vic anniversaries and that Old Vic diehards should resent the upstart National! How I wish I had been able to fully record Yolande's first-hand accounts of those eventful years.

The special performance involved creating a royal box, duly organised by a team from the Carpenters' Workshop, in the middle of the Dress Circle. To find suitable chairs for the official party I enlisted the help of the Props Master, Tommy Gillon - another great character. Unfortunately, I didn't set a budget for the chairs and remembered being shocked when presented with the hire bill. The evening went well. Jennie Lee as the Arts Minister attended and sat across the gangway from the Royal, Princess Marina. Everyone seemed to think it had been worth celebrating the occasion but I was amused to learn that the Minister's office had rung the morning after to check who it was who had occupied the special seats in the box area...

I really do regret not having made more notes about notable attendees I 'met' during this exciting period to the extent of organising interval refreshment or even just noticing them in the Box Office queue; I do recall I failed to identify Alec Guinness on one occasion, but then that was, of course, his skill! Nureyev came to many early performances after his defection, always late and having to be smuggled in contrary (again) to our ban on latecomers. Film stars, leading musicians and eminent public figures all made their way to Waterloo Road to enjoy the National's offerings. I discovered that I had many more Oxford acquaintances than I remembered when they tracked me down having met with no success booking tickets via regular channels.

Two people adopted me as their booking agent. Ralph Vaughan Williams' widow, Ursula, wrote to me in despair when faced with one of our booking systems and was a delight to help. After once looking after Sybil Thorndike at Sir's request, she also became one of my regular correspondents since I could find her tickets near the stage as 'poor Lewis really can't hear or see very well'. I think it was also through fulfilling similar Olivier instructions that I became the recipient of Sir Malcolm Sargeant's booking requests and learnt that he had been knighted at the same investiture as Olivier. These were usually straightforward requests and at the most a matter of accessing house tickets those concerned could have acquired anyway with a phone call. It was part of the job keeping everyone happy as far as I was concerned – and not per an instruction in a handbook.

Members of the National's board usually attended first nights *en masse*, perhaps otherwise they risked a note from our Chairman, Lord Chandos. He was a large man (and his wife was very thin by contrast - someone told me that unkindly they were referred to as 'beauty and the beast') and was always extremely courteous to everyone he met.

On one occasion his guest was Lord Drogheda, the chairman of Covent Garden, who was noticeably deferential to his host and with none of the airs later associated with his behaviour. I must say I always found him courteous to a fault when he came to the Coliseum in later years (remarking that our sandwiches were better than those at the ROH). Another guest was Jennie Lee, soon after the 1964 Labour election victory with a small majority, who arrived at the last minute full of apologies about Parliamentary pressures. "I remember those times" was the Chandos comment.

The first board members were certainly a distinguished group. The two Clarks - Kenneth (of 'Civilisation' fame) and Ashley (who campaigned for the restoration of Venice after the terrible floods of 1966) made particular impressions, as did 'Binkie' Beaumont. Some were a surprise to meet in the flesh when organising a drink for them at the bar. Henry Moore was the most surprising, looking and dressing just like a bank manager. Sir Bronson Albery, with his long association with the Old Vic company, was pleasant to look after at a performance, once I got to remember that his choice was *Irish* whiskey. There were occasional references to the Old Vic seasons at his New Theatre, but he didn't encourage extensive conversation.

Arlen had his own way of passing on professional guidance, as is probably already clear by now. As a former theatre and company manager himself (and very many other roles including Demon King in panto) his guidance to me was always succinct and to the point. I had been well drilled by Duggie at Sadler's Wells about showing my face to the audience front of house – 'walking the house'. In Arlen's view the theatre manager should also regularly visit every dressing room backstage and make his presence obvious so that comments, even complaints, could be made in person rather than fester and become the subject of a formal letter from Equity, the actors' union. This led to some interesting encounters with company members backstage: Max Adrian, a wonderful Inquisitor in *St Joan* – always anxious to gossip, Michael Redgrave wondering how to adjust his radiator, and many ribald exchanges with John Stride! Higher up the dressing room block there were Derek Jacobi and Michael Gambon to visit. Contact with leading ladies was a little more brief; perhaps it was just my age which made me very deferential to Joan Plowright or Maggie Smith. When *Hay Fever* was first in rep with the Master, Noel Coward, directing, and Edith Evans playing Judith Bliss, I avoided her dressing room lest I be held responsible for her fluffing even more of her lines than she regularly did. There had been a terrible moment when the programmes first arrived with one photograph captioned as Edith Adams. All staff were allocated black pens to block out that name pronto. No one ever owned up to failing to spot that on the programme proof.

Another memorable story of this production concerned Edith Evans' inability to get a line about seeing Marlow through the sitting room window clearly. The line was 'on a clear day you can see Marlow' but Edith at several rehearsals inserted 'very' before Marlow which led the Master to exclaim: " NO! On a very clear day you can see Beaumont and Fletcher!' On an easier level I enjoyed chats with Mary Miller who left the company after the first season but became a regular audience member with husband Bill Simpson of Dr Findlay's Casebook fame. The tiny canteen backstage was a great place to chat with the company though it could also be the place to be accosted for some housekeeping misdemeanour. I also took in the electricians'worshop/staff room on occasions where two staff members, John Read and Chris Arthur were to be found. The former became an eminent lighting designer for ballet while Chris moved on to be a very successful photographer.

There was one dressing room I <u>had</u> to visit if Sir was performing and I would duly make the trip to see him and deliver in person the box office return, a statement of the financial results of the performance. It took me a little while to get into the routine of pinpointing the right moment during a performance when he was off stage and when the return from the box office would be finalised and therefore available to deliver. When presented to Sir (who was normally, if I got the timing right, sitting at the roll top desk which had belonged to Lilian Baylis, in No 1 dressing room), it was important for him to know who was using the complimentary tickets - this was surely another hangover from actor manager days. Sometimes the guest's name would be unfamiliar to me as when I reported that a certain Jill Esmond was attending. 'My first wife' he reminded me. We had, I think, a couple of visits from Vivien Leigh (accompanied by Peter Finch) but I don't recall having to explain those tickets to Sir.

From the earliest days the National made efforts to accommodate younger audiences at reduced prices although this was a balancing act in financial terms. The Old Vic company had always given matinee performances for London schools, in those days organised by the Inner London Education Authority. Having seen myself how unruly such audiences could become at Rosebery Avenue (an auditorium full of nothing but schoolkids…) I set about persuading the ILEA office of the benefit of breaking the school parties down into smaller groups so there weren't large swathes seated together from the same school - the theory being that kids might be inhibited into good behaviour by having unfamiliar kids sat by them. Shock horror at the admin involved when put to the ILEA but eventually there was acceptance with successful results. After a while there were informal Q&A sessions after certain performances with two or three members of the cast which proved widely popular. (Another landmark theatre activity, now accepted as the norm!)

Such ILEA matinees were scheduled way ahead - sometimes before the production had entered rehearsal and revealed its nature. Such was the case with Peter Brook's *Oedipus*. When the graphic nature of Brook's production became clear, consultation with the ILEA led to the decision to end the performance before the procession on stage of a large phallic symbol on a plinth – which took place towards the end of the piece - and then to hold a discussion. The general reaction from the young audience was to ask 'what have we missed?' and why they had been deprived of seeing the rest of the show. I don't think we got any letters from parents, but at regular performances there were often audience members queueing up to berate management as they left! Some didn't last the performance and had to receive attention from our St John's Ambulance first aiders. I kept a note in a little book as to how many fainted, walked out or who were going to write to the Director/Chairman/their MP. Not sure what happened to that record. There were always patrons lined up to see the duty manager in the foyer after a performance to register comments such as *"outrageous", "disgusting", "shouldn't be allowed at the NATIONAL theatre".*

Peter Brook's production of Oedipus was memorable for many reasons. The procession of the phallic symbol was one, but when the audience entered the auditorium they found members of the company strapped to pillars in the stalls, balancing on specially fitted foot rests (that entailed special clearance from the GLC) so they immediately knew even if they hadn't caught the press comments that they were in for anything but a traditional interpretation. Stories abound about comments amongst the cast – was it John Gielgud who actually came out with 'Was the plinth, plinth Philip or plinth Charles'? It wasn't, though many ascribe it to Gielgud. Nor was it Gielgud who when responding to Brook's request to the company to tell him individually the worst thing they could, responded "we open in two f***ing weeks". That was Frank Wylie who was renowned for telling utterances! I had minimal contact with Brook at this time but I do recall he had a very penetrating look and searching blue eyes (just like Maurice Béjart).

New Audiences

Making tickets available at reduced prices to encourage new, predominantly young theatregoers was obviously an investment for the future – but it didn't help balance the books of the present. I had no idea how exactly it came about, but a grant in 1966 from the tobacco company, Carreras, enabled the National to set up 'New Audiences'- perhaps one of the first audience development schemes'. This allowed the blocking off of seats at certain evening performances which could be sold at reduced prices to particular groups ranging from sixth formers, youth clubs, training colleges to universities. In simple terms, providing the opportunity for those who might be unable to afford regular prices to see a wide range of plays. This was probably an early move by cigarette manufacturers to present an acceptable public face - but whatever the motivation it was a great success and hugely popular. The process of identifying the groups and making it all happen was down to Yolande - a real *tour de force*. I never learnt why exactly the scheme ended but after a mostly well supported five years, the National entered a period when the audience was not as populous as it had been and there was much talk by senior administration about getting a new audience (without capitals). A forceful exponent of this drive was Frank Dunlop.

In the first years of the National's existence Stephen Arlen had been on loan from Sadler's Wells Opera. We were informed in 1964 that he would be available for consultation as an adviser but otherwise he was returning to his role at the opera company. Shortly thereafter it seemed there was a palace revolution there and he became the MD. It was only as time passed I realised how he had chosen to be No 1 at the opera as opposed to No 2 at the National. Certainly he was widely respected by members of the National board and considered a good partner for Olivier. To most he also represented a continuation of the progress of activity at the Old Vic towards a National Theatre given his early work as general manager with the Old Vic Theatre School.

After Stephen returned to Sadler's Wells his work was initially undertaken by the production manager, George Rowbottom, who became General Manager. George was incredibly 'nice' but not of sufficient character (it seemed to the likes of staff like myself) to control, or persuade, Sir or the Associates John Dexter and Bill Gaskill. George eventually went off to run Nottingham Playhouse and Frank Dunlop arrived, initially as an Associate Director moving on to become Administrative Director in 1968.

Frank took up the cause of getting new audiences and let it be known that he thought the organisation should be less stuffy. This was fine but it soon became clear (to me) that what Frank really wanted was a separate strand of activity and this he achieved in 1969. Special Arts Council funding was given to the National to build a basic auditorium behind a former butcher's shop close to the Old Vic in the Cut which would cater specifically for young audiences. This was designated the

Young Vic (few realised that there had been a group of young players with this title operating under the aegis of the Old Vic Company in the late 1940s) and attracted much attention. The organisation eventually went on to a separate existence from the National and achieved great success. The initial structure (opened by the octogenarian Sybil Thorndike) which was intended to last no more than five years went on for many more years eventually being revamped in 2004-6 and becoming one of London's most popular young peoples' theatres.

The butcher's shop in The Cut which
became the Young Vic foyer

105

Beyond the Waterloo Road and The Grand Tour of 1967

International visitors beat a path to the National from its earliest days and I often found myself entertaining many eminent theatre visitors on Sir's behalf. At one stage the National was investigating a North American tour and David Merrick came to many performances. Also investigated, I gleaned, was a tour to Australia/New Zealand and Japan but this didn't get further than some exploratory work by Sunny Amey, the wonderful New Zealander who was Olivier's assistant for many years. There were many visits from theatre people from behind the Iron Curtain and it was revealing to hear their comments about the theatre scene in the GDR, Poland and Czechoslovakia. Contact with the latter brought Josef Svoboda to design *Three Sisters* and introduce an entirely new approach to stage design. In 1965 there was a tour to Moscow and then West Berlin, not the easiest routing. The US part of an American tour plan didn't happen but the National did go to Canada for the Centennial in 1967, working there with an Australian publicist - David Palmer - with whom Sir was much taken and who was later to join the National staff.

Besides VIPs, I was often asked to 'look after' international visitors whose tickets had been organised by the International Theatre Institute (ITI). The ITI was another of the attempts post-WWII to promote international harmony with a brief to 'promote international exchange of knowledge and practice in theatre arts'. The British Centre of the ITI was headed by Kenneth Rae (who had been a publisher before the war and associated with the ITI organisation since its founding in Prague in 1947). He was ably assisted by Yolande Bird. Both of them performed these roles in addition (with very little financial return I suspect) to their roles at the National (Rae was the Board Secretary). I was often asked to say hello to their visitors and perhaps find them a programme or drink. In doing so, I gradually picked up quite a bit of information about world theatre!

From 1964 to 1973 while the RSC took a short summer break from giving performances at the Aldwych, the impresario Peter Daubeney presented a World Theatre Season and gave Londoners some memorable theatre experiences. In the interests of theatre harmony members of these overseas companies were usually invited to mid-week matinees (Thursday at the Old Vic, so avoiding the Wednesday matinee at the Aldwych) and given tea after the show with one or two National company members attending. Sometimes jolly and other times near disaster as when a Greek company came without any interpreter.

As a result of these activities and associated conversations with Yolande, I developed a desire to see more of theatre activity abroad. The prompt for this was the discussion which occasionally came my way about the new National Theatre building on the South Bank comprising several auditoria and common foyers. How would all this be managed and how would things be organised? I badgered

Kenneth Rae to know what was in the brief to Denys Lasdun for the new theatre and eventually learnt there were many open questions about how the two auditoria would operate on a practical basis as far as audiences were concerned. After seeing a television programme about Gelsenkirchen's new theatre I started taking a particular interest in the seeming multitude of theatres being built in West Germany many of which, I thought, could provide lessons. Aided by Yolande I applied to the Arts Council for a bursary to go on a visit; much to my surprise my single page letter (those were the days!) met with success.

This led to serious planning. After a meeting with the redoubtable Dr Brigitte Lohmeyer, cultural officer at the West German Embassy, I sought on her advice guidance from the renowned expert in theatre architecture, Victor Glasstone. Our initial encounter at his tiny Paddington flat crammed with filing cabinets did not get off to a good start when I revealed I wasn't a German speaker. He was nonetheless a great help in providing me with suggestions of places to visit. Many years later when Sue and I visited him at his hilltop castello outside Lucca in Italy and I reminded him of his attitude to my lack of German, he revealed that he had spent a lot of time when in the GDR speaking with such strong emphasis in Afrikaans (he being South African) that he convinced those he addressed that he was using German. It was Victor who led to my being a collector of theatre postcards. After my tour, when he quite often came as my guest to a performance, he saw the cards from other visitors on my office notice board and thereafter invariably communicated on a postcard featuring a theatre.

My grand tour was made in two parts – partly because of not wanting to leave the Old Vic for too long (how would my assistant -by now St John Sandringham – possibly cope?) – and partly to make the travelling around easier. My bursary did not extend to any flights, so making sense of railway schedules required much input from an old style travel agent, the wonderful Mr Clark who operated out of a tiny office crammed with timetables just off Trafalgar Square.

First stop was the Netherlands where my visits were brilliantly planned by the ITI office. I stayed in the Hague and travelled out by very efficient Dutch railways to the various venues I had been advised to see. Whilst nearly everyone spoke perfect English the announcements at railway stations were pretty difficult to follow and changing trains at Hertogenbosch filled me with awe until I was firmly told the train would arrive at my destination at exactly 11.23 and that's when you get off. It did and I did.

I found that in Holland as the theatre was organised on touring lines (companies travelled out from their home bases for, in effect, a series of one night stands), the buildings needed to be able to accommodate everything from large scale classics to intimate review. So most towns had two auditoria to provide an appropriate setting for whatever was on offer. There were many new buildings and very often a studio to supplement the main auditorium space. From the very beginning of my visits I couldn't fail to notice the space given over to audiences - especially in respect of spaces to hang coats. Nothing like the tiny cubby holes I was used to in London, with long waits to retrieve articles after the show. The other particular note I made about Dutch discussions was that a government committee of architects and theatre professionals existed to vet new theatre proposals on grounds of <u>need</u> rather than civic pride. Two vastly contrasting notes amongst many impressions from a packed week visiting Amsterdam, Eindhoven, Nijmegen, Rotterdam, Tilburg and The Hague.

After my various Dutch visits I moved on to Brussels where Stephen Arlen had arranged for me to meet with the head of La Monnaie. Whilst this famous old opera house was not the kind of new multi-auditorium venue I was especially interested in, its director, Maurice Huisman, was clearly a man with ideas and energy, as I later discovered when he brought Bejart's Ballet of the 20th Century to London. I also met his brother Jacques, who was running the French speaking drama company in two auditoria located in a tower block (which also housed a Martini Terrace such as then existed in London's New Zealand House) but not with the same 'try anything' approach as his brother. Arlen had been involved with the Monnaie at one stage when newly-appointed Maurice was trying to reinvigorate it as an opera house – they certainly had similar approaches! I believe they had met during the war when Huisman was involved with the resistance. Arlen was an officer in the North Staffordshire regiment.

Although the Monnaie was certainly grand the Brussels theatre which made the most impression in 1967 was the Theatre Royal du Parc, an 18th century building on the edge of the park around the royal palace. It was impressive but had no second space so no message other than it was (then) well cared for!

After Brussels came Paris where I took in the national houses of Comedie Francaise, Theatre de L'Odeon and Palais de Chaillot as well as Theatre de l'Est Parisien. No particular striking memories as I recall of those large buildings and officialdom... but I did get told a lot about how wonderful the *maison de la culture* concept was; it was not until my time at a Pearle conference in Basel that I saw one in action (actually managed by an Englishman, Christopher Crimes) in 1996.

After a brief spell of duty back at the Old Vic, I set off for the next series of visits, taking in Bonn, Frankfurt, Gelsenkirchen, Kassel, Solingen, Stuttgart, Wuppertal and West Berlin. My theatre visits were arranged by an organisation which I believe was government funded, Internationes. Needless to add the visits were all extremely efficiently organised and I saw some very modern buildings (both impressive and not so impressive) and met with a variety of administrators. The surprise to me was that some of these characters could be moving on to running the local hospital; rarely, I recall, were they theatre people through and through. But the modern buildings were certainly well run and, as I insisted on visiting as much of their buildings as possible, tolerant of my tape recorder and camera. The most uncomfortable experience was in West Berlin where I was taken to view the infamous wall and look across to the derelict Reichstag and learn of the fate of those who had attempted to cross the wall. I returned to the UK via Copenhagen where I toured the Royal Theatre and its 1930 'new stage'.

Fuelled by all I had seen on the continent I set about making one modest but immediate change at the Old Vic in cloakroom arrangements. We simply booked all the FOH staff to man a set of mobile coat racks. These were loaded with hats and coats in the cloakroom cubby hole during the incoming, with the staff handing them back out to their owners in the empty stalls bar at the end of the show. That brought a few kind remarks from patrons who had thus been saved a lot of queueing.

There was a further arrangement in many of the theatres I had visited which had caught my attention and that related to how seats were numbered. In those days UK patrons were taken to their seats by usherettes who knew just how the row numbers were set out but as curtain up approached this led to difficulty and queues formed as patrons waited to be shown their seats. I decided to change the Old Vic's seat numbering to the continental system, whereby the auditorium had a centre line and numbers increased or decreased either side so the shorter rows wouldn't start with number one. (Another continental practice which I did not install at the Vic was to use the central gangway -where it existed – to separate even and uneven numbered seats, so patrons could be directed to even or uneven numbered seats.) We also labelled the theatre aisles so the staff had a clearer idea of where seats were. I drove our ticket printers mad adding directional information onto every ticket so that our ushers simply had to read that to the patron and let them follow the labels we had installed around the auditorium. It was this kind of information that I always asked the computer experts when they came along to supply but of course this didn't take account of how fast technology would develop making such detail unnecessary (eg hand held readers for theatre staff). In my wildest dreams I had no idea that one day theatres would completely dispense with a box office as such, as is now the case at Theatre Royal Drury Lane following its 2022 transformation.

My report to the Arts Council about my findings took a little longer to achieve than did the physical changes at the Waterloo Road - perhaps because I asked Yolande to vet it, leading to many "but what do you really mean?" sessions over glasses of wine.

Sue and I drove through France to Italy that summer of 1967 and when we returned from holiday I had a pleasant surprise: an invitation to attend the Berlin Festival in the GDR! This, I think, had come my way because Yolande - to whom the invitation had been sent originally - was unable to accept for personal reasons. Although I had no particular knowledge of board politics I think it was around this time that the Rolf Hochhuth play, *Soldiers*, was beginning to arouse controversy; word filtered down that there had been heated rows between the board and Olivier and Tynan. The all-male production of *As You Like It* also certainly created its own heated discussions that October. The programme for the production contained in true Ken Tynan fashion a number of provocative illustrations which were soon to give me some unsettling encounters in the GDR.

Leaving behind the boardroom dramas at the Vic, I once again set off from Harwich and crossed to the Hook of Holland where I joined the train for Berlin. Although I had travelled across the GDR from Stuttgart to West Berlin earlier in the year without incident, this trip saw very thorough checks on board as we crossed West Berlin to Friedrichstrasse in East Berlin. I can still remember the barriers and myriads of officials on the platform as I got off a train which had obviously somehow survived the war (just). My briefcase was of course full of papers about our new National Theatre with a number of programmes to hand out to my hosts. I had adopted this practice on my earlier visits and, as the material seemed to have been appreciated, I assumed it would go down as well with my communist hosts. However, after asking me to open my briefcase on the platform, an official flicked through the *As You Like It* programme (complete with provocative images) and, with stern face, immediately ordered me into a private room for further interrogation; it was only when I produced my official invitation to the Berlin Festival with its impressive GDR heading that I was eventually allowed to make my way to my exceptionally modest hotel in Unter den Linden - not by any stretch of the imagination a branch of the Adlon!

In West Berlin at the infamous Wall during my 1967 visit

After this terrifying introduction the visit went calmly with impressive performances at the Staatsoper and Komische Oper. The latter was perhaps the most memorable since the approach to *Bluebeard's Castle* taken by director Walter Felsenstein was such fun and the whole atmosphere of the Komische such a contrast to the general greyness elsewhere in the city. I had some free time to visit museum island (much was still closed and awaiting restoration) but of course there was an obligatory session learning about how the wall was protecting citizens from bad influences.

My invitation included a visit to Leipzig to take in a visit to their new opera house – a vast building where I saw a *Don Carlos* in which the *auto da fe* took place in a large rear stage and, it seemed, a street behind! I remember thinking the building looked like a large fortress perhaps because it was the background to a military style youth rally the day after my visit to *Don Carlos*. When I returned to Leipzig in 2016 the whole area seemed to be rather more human although the opera house foyers were even more extensive than I remembered them.

I have to confess I was rather glad to be back in London after that trip.

Back at the Vic we had Tyrone Guthrie directing Tartuffe and Volpone. Guthrie was a larger than life character – he was well over six foot tall and always seemed to be wearing carpet slippers when I saw him in the Aquinas Street offices. His productions weren't that popular (even with Gielgud in *Tartuffe*) but he did share stories of the Minneapolis theatre with a select group of us one evening, made even more enjoyable by input from legendary theatre designer Tanya Moiseiwitsch. It was while Guthrie was working with the National that Sue found herself designing an ad for the jams his 'factory' in Eire produced – typical of the man that he had set up this enterprise to give locals much needed employment.

I have already referred to one of the notable productions of 1968, Seneca's *Oedipus*. Directed by Peter Brook it brought more than its share of drama, not necessarily on stage. There were obviously many heated discussions in Dressing Room 1 (Olivier's) post-rehearsals since I had to have the large mirror on the back of the door replaced on at least two occasions.

The same year - 1968 - brought much student unrest around Europe during which time we hosted guest performances by the Renault Barrault company whose base at the Odeon was in the midst of the Paris rioting. I recall there being one quote (in the Times) which proclaimed *'today l'Odeon, tomorrow the Old Vic"*. We also had a taste of Beatlemania when John Lennon's *In His Own Write* was part of a triple bill. Audience reaction was quite modest compared to *Oedipus*!

London display of support

About 250 students marched along Oxford Street in London last night in support of the French students. They chanted slogans such as " De Gaulle out ". " Students and workers unite and fight " and " Occupy the banks ", and carried placards saying "Down with the bourgeoisie " and " Today l'Odéon, tomorrow the Old Vic ".

The demonstration was organized by the National Association of Labour Student Organizations. Mr. George Myers, aged 22, a student at Oriel College, Oxford, and secretary of the association, said they wanted the same thing to happen in Britain as had happened in France, with the workers taking over the factories and the students the universities. " There will be rioting and violence in the streets but we are not going to start it ", he said.

A cutting from The Times from the days of the 1968 riots in Paris

For me, the most significant event of that summer was elsewhere: the first performance by Sadler's Wells Opera at the Coliseum on August 21 (sadly coinciding with Soviet tanks rolling into Prague). I had kept in touch with one or two colleagues at the Wells so knew something of Arlen's desire to find a West End home once the plan for a new building for the opera company was removed from the South Bank scheme. After the Coliseum announcement, Sue and I went to see the Cinerama offering there; it had been a cinema for some while and though a young Sue had been taken there to see *Cinderella* with Tommy Steele, I had never crossed the threshold. I don't remember much about the film (except that at one stage the projectors were out of sync) but I do remember us wandering into the bars below the foyer which appeared as if they were part of a Sleeping Beauty set, complete with cobwebs. It was therefore with a sense of wonderment at the transformation in the building that we attended the first night of *Don Giovanni* - not, in my opinion, a great triumph for John Gielgud's direction nor (especially) for Derek Jarman, the designer!

I think it was the publicity that surrounded the opera at the Coliseum that set me assessing where I stood career-wise. After all, I had been at the National for six years and was approaching my mid-life crisis at the age of twenty nine! I had had a couple of conversations with Arlen after he had left the National and when I seemed to be stuck in a rut at the Vic (impatience of youth!), and even had an interview with Sir David Webster at Covent Garden for a post 'looking after Sir Fred' (Ashton) but that didn't excite me and I obviously didn't appeal to them. The interview was memorable for Webster's PA asking him what he wanted for lunch before we began; they got their priorities right at the Opera House. I suppose I really hankered after something to do with publicity but at the National that was always a strange area. Technically, Tynan was responsible for the public image of the National and for Virginia Fairweather, the Press Representative, but I certainly did a lot of what might be considered publicity work with ordering posters and leaflets and involvement in their design. One knew from asides from critics and the then pre-eminent Sunday Times Arts Correspondent, Kenneth Pearson, that Virginia was rather better at keeping the press away than assisting (a hangover perhaps from her days protecting Olivier in the difficult period when the Vivien Leigh marriage was failing). Even when Virginia was eventually replaced by David Palmer, the National was not a place where you moved sideways – one got the impression that Sir didn't like the established order being disturbed.

For our summer holiday in 1969 Sue and I retraced the steps we had taken for the previous 3 years and I drove down to Positano and then onto and around Sicily. In those days Sue did not drive and looking back I am amazed at my stamina (which included driving up to Inverness for a wedding and back in a weekend). The Sicily trip was in the days of financial restrictions (a £50 limit for all your holiday spending abroad, as I recall) but we were lucky in being able to pay sterling for our stay in – then – unspoilt Positano where the owner's wife was English and happy to take a sterling cheque. We reckoned we could just about meet the costs for the rest of the trip via some dollars being mailed to Naples from the US by an Oxford chum, Nick Fisher. These were to await our return to Naples on the ferry from Palermo. We did achieve this but not without a hair-raising early morning moment in the Naples post office: the name Rhymes has a lot of letters unusual for Italians, quite apart from my rather fraught attempts at adapting schoolboy Latin to explain I was due to receive a very important letter from USA. Finally the envelope was produced and had it not been early morning I think we would have downed several glasses of vino.

Sharing a drink with some of the Old Vic catering staff after my last evening as Theatre Manager, October 1969

The journey down the boot of Italy in our tiny Hillman Imp took us through areas still very rural and often our drive through little more than tracks was probably the wonder of the year for locals, especially with a car which had luggage stored at the front. The tourist hot spots of Sicily were definitely 'on the map' and we managed to fit in an impressive number. Taormina was of course included (how could it not be with that theatre?) and lived in our memory as we got drenched by a torrential downpour and had to resort to changing in the car. We didn't manage to see more of the great opera house in Palermo than its exterior – renovation in progress – but many years later we achieved a full tour and a performance and appreciated what a mammoth undertaking its restoration had been. Sue was always very patient as every amphitheatre or town theatre was duly photographed or a postcard sought.

My rather pretentious change of address
card when I left the Old Vic

Back in London, a welcome job change came about after a session with Arlen who I think was by now worn down by my enquiries about possibilities at the Coliseum. He offered me a job as assistant to the Administrative Director, Edward Renton - no precise job description and a lot of vagueness about what it might lead to. This wasn't a route I would expect anyone to consider for a moment these days but there was then a buzz about the Coli and indeed Arlen himself. So the appropriate letters were written and I started a new life with the opera on October 8 1969. There were some very jovial farewells with the staff at the Vic, many of the front of house team were almost family and there are some photos to remind me of the emotional departure. I also received a very warm note from the Chairman, Chandos and from Olivier – (there was even a vote of thanks proposed by Chandos recorded in the Board minutes apparently) - all in the files still, somewhere!

WEST
END TRANSFER

The London Coliseum seen from Trafalgar Square

I recall feeling rather lost in my early days working for Edward at the Coliseum; he wasn't very clear as to what I should be doing and though I read a lot of files and tried to understand his approach to 'negotiation' I don't think I learned a great deal. It was not helped by my feeling that the front of house management left a lot to be desired. The opera had taken a ten year lease of the building from the owners, Stoll Theatres Corporation, headed by a very commercial West End theatre character, Prince Littler, with whom Arlen had a certain rapport as he had worked for him at various stages in his career. This relationship no doubt played a significant part in securing the Coliseum lease. (Arlen was always referred to by Littler as 'Ocky' having once played Octavius in a Littler production of *The Barrets of Wimpole Street*). Part of the deal was that the theatre manager, Raymond Lane, moved on to the opera payroll but also looked after the landlord's interests. Raymond was steeped in commercial theatre having managed various venues in the regions before coming to London. Understandably his approach to dealing with both public and staff bore more affinity to what I had seen at the Aldwych than at Sadler's Wells. I did persuade him to give me an introductory tour of the theatre which showed me what an incredible building Frank Matcham had created and initiated my interest in both its history and the man himself.

I cultivated relationships with long standing employees such as the house engineer, Con Watkins, who introduced me to the wonders of the under stage revolve machinery. Behind a solid wall below the stage was housed a labyrinth of girders which it was still possible to walk through, though the revolve itself had long ceased to function. The story was that it ran on direct current electricity, the supply of which had ended when London trams had been withdrawn from service. Some claimed – perhaps correctly – that it had been operational when the opera company gave operetta seasons at the Coliseum in 1958/9. This vast space remained unused until we found the money to convert it for staff use many years later.

When the Coliseum was in use as a cinema many areas were let to provide income. Most noticeable at the front of the building for a long time was the Admiral's Eye gift shop occupying a space which had, I believe, once been part of the booking office. Behind the iron curtain large parts of the stage area were used by a local builder, while a section of dressing rooms functioned as commercial offices with a separate entrance onto May's Court which runs up the side of the building. These Arlen managed to secure from Littler and they were swiftly returned to dressing room use apart from those offices which were used by Arlen himself and the technical administration. In order to provide the necessary office accommodation initially a lease had been taken on the property next door to the theatre, 31 St Martin's Lane. This building had been the HQ of Prince Littler's brother, Emile Littler, the producer of very successful pantomimes (having cornered this particular market in much the same way as producer Paul Elliott did for thirty years from the sixties). In order to ease communication for the opera personnel, a high level bridge connection (over what was then a very smelly alleyway, now an acceptable walkway) was made between the theatre and no 31. It transpired at the time of the major restoration in 2004 that there had been no official approval for this; perhaps just another story! A final addition to accommodation for the opera company was the lease of a Victorian warehouse up the alleyway under the bridge which had been Westminster Council's Rodent Operatives' Depot. It inevitably became known as Ratcatchers.

As the days passed and my attention turned to how things were organised I found myself thinking that besides better house management, the other area which might benefit from my attention was that of promotion – press and publicity. Arlen had decided to experiment with the move to the Coli by appointing a Marketing Manager (this was way before the title was widespread in theatre life) and setting up a new form of supporters' organisation. At both the Vic and Sadler's Wells, the Vic Wells Association, dating back to Lilian Bayliss's days, operated as a supporters' club for both organisations, but was definitely not part of the formal structure. Arlen felt it should be possible to attract the interest and active support of supporters and direct them in a more meaningful way than coffee mornings and meet the cast sessions. Thus was born 'The Opera Club'. Arlen recruited two young (around my age!) characters: Eric Reynolds as Marketing Manager and Richard Phillips as the Opera Club Manager. There was a lot of buzz – and jargon - associated with these two. Eric used an advertising agency to advise on the best use of the publicity budget and they came up with some interesting approaches - half page advertisements in the London Evening Standard with provocative texts. These certainly provoked comment but the ad with "all opera singers aren't fat" at the time when the amply proportioned Rita Hunter featured in a number of productions was a little unfortunate to say the least.

The Opera Club initially attracted a lot of attention offering a mixture of events in the same vein as many theatre organisations do nowadays, under the 'outreach' banner. Richard also edited the magazine which had replaced the *Repertoire* newspaper (the brainchild of a former press officer). Strangely, Arlen did not make radical changes in the way the press were managed. In his early days as Managing Director he had recruited Edmund Tracey from The Observer to fill a role at Sadler's Wells similar to that of Tynan at the National, though their characters were poles apart. Edmund had picked up Arlen's early work in changing the printed image of the company and used two graphic designers to oversee how the opera company was seen in print. To me it was strange that he accepted the advertising agency 'interpretation' of the house style since it bore little relation to the house style he clearly believed in. Edmund also oversaw the press office, run by a very efficient lady, Helen Salomon, who viewed her domain as entirely separate from any other part of the administration only answerable, occasionally, to the Managing Director and certainly not co-ordinating with that 'marketing lot'!

So there was quite a lot for me to look at and think how it might be improved, besides trying to follow Edward's approach to admin. There was also quite a lot to think about as far as the gossip about the organisation of the company was concerned. Soon after my arrival it was announced that the two companies (Sadlers and Wells) which had technically existed at the time of the move would merge but at the end of the London season they would divide with one taking rep to larger venues and the other smaller pieces to towns with smaller theatres.

My first experience of a new production designed for the Coliseum was of *Patience* with a marvellous Bunthorne by Derek Hammond Stroud. There was also a small but delightful accompanying exhibition across the road at the National Portrait Gallery, then under the direction of Roy Strong. The Christmas production of the specially commissioned *Lucky Peter's Journey* (composer Malcolm Williamson, Master of the Queen's Music), was not such a happy experience. The special preview for the Greater London Arts Association with their patron Sir Ralph Richardson in attendance, was something of an embarrassment (poor story and certainly not catchy music) and performances remained sparsely attended despite a major and expensive television campaign.

1970 got off to a flying start as, on Jan 1, Charles Mackerras became Music Director. Even to my untrained ear there was a marked difference in the sound coming out of the pit. The general feeling was that everyone was on their best behaviour with far less depping when Mackerras was conducting. As time passed I gained invaluable information about how the orchestra worked and what they thought of Mackerras from the orchestral manager, Charles Coverman, who had a wealth of stories about working with Beecham. Mackerras also brought his own ructions, the first being his complaint that principals didn't take a bow at the end of each act, anathema to Arlen with his belief in musical theatre.

Later in January came *The Valkyrie*. It was only later that I learned just what a battle it had been to get the idea of an English Ring accepted by the committee which had been set up to 'co-ordinate' the repertoire of Covent Garden and Sadler's Wells with, apparently, an agreement that there should be a four month separation between performances of the same opera. Even the Arts Council now chaired by Lord Goodman had taken some convincing, initially suggesting that *The Valkyrie* might be seen as just an experiment. In the event the production was a triumph for all concerned. Reginald Goodall the conductor had already earned many plaudits for his work with the company on *Mastersingers* (he was actually still a member of the music staff at Covent Garden but was rather neglected there). Glen Byam Shaw and John Blatchley were the producers - much admired by the company for their patient approach - whilst design was in the hands of Ralph Koltai. He had already shown audiences his work with modern materials for the all-male *As You Like It* at the Old Vic for the National. His setting for *The Valkyrie* was apparently inspired by the recent moon landings... Rita Hunter and Alberto Remedios had particular triumphs.

Our post wedding lunch at the Post Office Tower, June 1970
L-R: Sue's father, my father, Sue, Sue's mother, self, my mother

I think it appropriate at this point to give a personal update. By the time of my move to the Coliseum, Sue and I were very much an 'item' and in June 1970 we decided that things should be formalised. Neither of us fancied any grand ceremony so a session with just our respective parents at Harrow Road Registry Office, followed by lunch in the revolving restaurant at the Post Office Tower, established Mr and Mrs Rhymes. We then went off to Corfu and the then little-known Paxos from which we sent a series of holiday postcards with the P.S. that we had got married...

At the Coli my reports with reorganisation proposals had been accepted and I was given the job of running the whole publicity and marketing operation. Since I clearly had less radical ideas of promotion than Eric, he decided to move on.

The Opera Club was deemed to be a financial commitment too far and Richard also sought pastures new. There were some strong supporters amongst the club members and at a 'protest' gathering it was agreed that the club should continue but be run by volunteers with no staff or financial company involvement. A number of opera fans came forward. One, Peter Francis, turned out to have reopened the Teatro di San Carlo in Naples during his WWII service. A travel agent in his civilian life, he was later to organise the opera company's visit to Vienna. A working committee was formed with one family, the Arratoons, taking a lead. They, with many others, gave splendid support for many years, the club eventually developing into the Friends (now ENO Friends); far from being a net cost, the new volunteer-run Friends were even able to make financial contributions to the company. In the Press Office, Helen Salomon, noted my appointment as her overlord but ploughed on in much the same way as previously. Since this efficiently got the company's message to the press this was fine except for some tricky and noisy moments when different approaches were called for... but we managed.

One of my first challenges in my new role was a promotion Arlen had arranged with Martini. The drinks company were then involved in a series of sporting and racing events as a way of promoting their brand – the early days of SPONSORSHIP! Arlen told me he wanted them to get a lot of prominent publicity whereas – in a reversal of the usual such situation – the person running Martini affairs in London (an ex-military character, Major Coverton) was for a more restrained presence. I had to carefully reconcile the two approaches. The production with which they were associated was that of *Carmen* - the first of many John Copley (production) and Stefan Lazaridis (design) partnerships - which was a great box office success. The deal was that Martini gave the opera company a big cheque (which certainly gave an extra boost to my budget), paid for extra publicity (with prominent Martini logo, of course) and in return received a number of tickets for their guests who went off to supper after the show at New Zealand House. Interesting looking back how much of a new departure this all was...

September 1970 saw the first signs of industrial unrest which would come to a head a few years later. My colleagues and I were aware of some of the difficulties the company's repertoire pattern of performing gave as far as ensuring the same technical crew were always available for a production, but there were also other issues. A roster pattern of work had been negotiated at the ROH and various attempts had been made with the rather ineffectual technicians' union, NATTKE, to achieve similar at the Coliseum. During the summer an agreement was finally reached with the union, but this was rejected by the staff who had not been consulted and saw less overtime coming their way even if the basic wage was higher. In early September negotiations broke down and the staff struck after curtain up on a *Carmen* performance when the crew (with a new steward and committee) learnt their union had once again struck a deal without consulting them. Not that surprising!

Olivier, fresh from playing Shylock (centre), with
Stephen Arlen (left) and his wife Iris Kells (right)

Frankly it was difficult for middle management like myself to grasp all the facts but we responded to the call to keep performances going. Without technical staff there were some strange settings (in one instance using some FOH bench seats since only sets already physically in the theatre were meant be used. This brought the comment from Glen Byam Shaw to Margaret Harris that the stage looked 'too spotty'. All performers worked as normal (whatever they may have thought privately). There was one furtive night time raid on the scenery stores for additional scenery, which was almost thwarted when the lorry was discovered to have flat tyres. I remember that those of us who provided muscle power moving furniture around enjoyed some delicious food provided by Arlen's wife, the soprano Iris Kells, –

probably the first time we got at all acquainted though she was not one to pull rank as the boss's wife.

Eventually an agreement was hammered out based on the ROH shift roster pattern. At the time Arlen considered it very satisfactory but I later came across a memo in which he claimed he had been misled about how the shifts allowed staff to log up vast overtime or earn large sums elsewhere on their supposed 'rest days' when they were not working at the Coliseum. As was later made clear, shifts with 15 ½ hour days weren't exactly conducive to productivity. Normal service was resumed in mid October.

I was aware from my 1967 Grand Tour that continental opera houses frequently mixed musicals as well as light opera and operettas with the traditional opera repertoire. Arlen felt that should also happen at the Coliseum and *Kiss Me Kate* was chosen for the Christmas offering in 1970. I was unaware at the time of any board misgivings or indeed of the suspicions of some West End managements that we were moving into their territory by presenting such a well-known musical (such insights emerged later). I did have the fun of meeting the piece's authors, Sam and Bella Spewack who had created the piece with Cole Porter and came over for a press launch. Quite a pair! Many memories were reignited about the previous production in 1951, which Spewack had himself directed at the Coliseum, achieving a good run of four hundred performances. Our new production opened on Christmas Eve and, whilst not the crowd puller Arlen had hoped for, it was certainly more popular with the public than the previous year's *Lucky Peter's Journey* and had a respectable revival at the start of the following season with strong performances from Anne Howard and Emile Belcourt.

When the opera season ended we welcomed a number of visiting companies. At the time of the announcement of the move to the Coliseum it had been stated that London Festival Ballet (with a new artistic director, Beryl Grey, taking over from Donald Albery), would give seasons at certain times. In addition to these regular appearances there were a number of one-off seasons. 1971 saw the first of what was to become several seasons of Maurice Bejart's, Ballet of the Twentieth Century. This company was resident at the Monnaie in Brussels and therefore under the general direction of Maurice Huisman. He had known Stephen Arlen for many years, having hired him as a consultant on taking over the theatre. As noted earlier, Huisman shared many of Arlen's characteristics and was always wanting to try new approaches not always backed by his devoted administrator, Anita Lotsy – which also fitted in with Bejart's view that ballet was theatre and a means of communication.

Although with a classical background and strong belief in the value of classical ballet, Bejart vehemently rejected its conventions: his dancers, for example, never wore tutus. For the first season at the Coliseum (Arlen had previously invited Bejart to bring his *Rite of Spring* to Sadler's Wells in 1960 as part of an exchange with the Monnaie), Huisman wanted a new form of promotion and hired an agency with as far as

I recall no entertainment background. The season launch/ press reception was on a boat on the Thames with wine served by very presentable females in the then-fashionable hot pants - not exactly Bejart style! The press coverage was poor and Huisman swiftly reverted to traditional methods! As a result I found myself much involved in placing ads/ posters and general promotion while Sue, by now a freelance graphic designer, was drawn in on the design side. Whilst administration was brilliantly handled by Anita Lotsy (who had travelled extensively with the company and was devoted to Huisman), there was a certain amount of informality about the company and those who travelled with it. The photographer Claire Falcy took some great shots but wasn't official in any way and arrived on the Coliseum doorstep without warning asking for a dark room to prepare prints for a display. The season turned out to be a great success and there was immediate talk about a return visit – they came back in '72, '74 and '77 to great public acclaim, under the slogan *'Bejart is back'* but we were in trouble if we referred to the Bejart Ballet. As far as Bejart - and indeed Huisman - was concerned it was a company and a style, the personality of the director was incidental.

The summer of 1971 also saw the design school which had been established under Margaret Harris' direction (Motley) mounting their end of year exhibition at the Coliseum understage around the wall of the revolve machinery. An event significant in my mind for logging up both what potential space there was and the incredible work of the design school. With no public funding, Margaret Harris, known throughout the profession as 'Percy', relied on leading professional directors and designers generously giving their time to teach a group of ten or eleven students from diverse backgrounds and countries. I was delighted to become more involved as a trustee years later working alongside John Simpson the founder (with other ex colleagues from the Royal Court) of White Light, the leading theatre technical supplier. I am sure John was a hidden sponsor of the Design School throughout its existence.

1971 also saw the Coliseum serve as the headquarters for the 14th International Congress of the ITI, a crowded week from May 29 to June 5. Arlen had recently become Chairman of the British Centre of the ITI and was a forceful participant in the business of the Musical Theatre Committee where he formed a warm relationship with Professor Walter Felsenstein (some of whose operetta productions I had hugely enjoyed in East Berlin). The main memory I have of the event was the constant fear of Yolande (who was the organising force) that there would be some major East/ West political incident – these were the iron curtain days when care had to be taken over how regimes were or were not recognised. The 200 or so delegates who descended on London from 46 countries were probably more interested in seeing the sights than making political waves! There were some rather special social events during the week – Lord Goodman hosted a reception at the Arts Council HQ at

105 Piccadilly complete with military band, and there was a formal dinner for 'senior' delegates in London's Guildhall hosted by the Lord Mayor of London with 'others' like myself dining at the Garrick Club (I think my first visit). To be honest there were no earth shattering conclusions from the conference but I certainly met some interesting characters and found the experience of being involved in a small way in its organisation useful for the future.

As had become the norm, the next season started in August ('Only Sadler's Wells has opera in August' was an advertising line for a while). The 1971/2 season's first new production was *Lohengrin* produced by Colin Graham and followed by a modern dress *Cavalleria rusticana and Pagliacci* (*Cav and Pag*) produced by John Blatchley. Colin was one for involvement in all aspects of his productions and certainly took an interest in the publicity but was not always easy to deal with. I only really formed a good relationship with him some years later when I became interested in his project for a West End health club and we discussed the practicalities of building management. At the time, though, it was hard to get any information from John about how he was conceiving his shows. (He always pressed Sue for a poster of his production – 'for the loo wall at home' apparently). For *Cav & Pag* it took much pressing from me to get his slant on the animosity of the protagonists in the contemporary Italian village and unfortunately many critics were annoyed by details – such as the car trailer which was seen as anachronistic. They were more receptive to David

Pountney's car scrapyard version years later!

Working for Arlen was never straightforward or routine. There were some surprising incursions into the run of opera performances at his behest: for example, as '71 progressed there was a 'one night stand' of a concert by the Israeli Philharmonic Orchestra which occasioned my meeting the renowned agent, Emmie Tillett. On another occasion, prompted by a comment that "people just don't understand how an opera is put together", he decided we should rectify this by staging 'The Elements of Opera'. However informative and entertaining this evening was for the audience, it took an awful lot of work to create. There were also concerts on stage and transmitted by BBC Radio (*Sunday Night at the London Coliseum*) as another way of 'diversifying'. Finally, I was involved in highly interesting negotiations involving representatives of Great Ormond Street Hospital and the Tom Arnold management about a season at Christmas of *Peter Pan*.

The run of *Kiss Me Kate* had not been the hoped-for financial success and Arlen believed a series of matinee performances with one or two evenings by an outside company would not only provide income but allow the opera company some time off as well as rehearsal time for *The Ring*. When Goodall heard of the plans, not realising the separate nature of what was intended he apparently wrote to Arlen expressing concern that the amply proportioned Rita Hunter might miss his *Valkyrie* rehearsals because of her involvement with Peter Pan! (Arlen conducted skilful correspondence with Goodall which, while comparing notes about their various gardening activities, allowed him to work in occasional bad news such as impossibility of granting more rehearsal time).

I attended various meetings with Helen and Tom Arnold (the widow and son of the highly successful impresario with identical name) gathering something of the complexities of the copyright for *Peter Pan* given by the author to Great Ormond Street Hospital, who had recently ended the licence for the Daniel Mayer Company to mount productions. A deal was struck and the Arnolds set about engaging Robert Helpmann to mount a new production with Dorothy Tutin and Eric Porter. So the scene was set for regular seasons of *Peter Pan* at the Coliseum, not always popular with my management colleagues after Arlen's death. Indeed, there were years when I would start the process of telling the Arnold office to seek another theatre only to be told to confirm a further season as we needed the money... which lasted until 1974.

By now I was involved in the company's tour planning and it was in this connection that I got to know another remarkable theatre person, Pat Bancroft. In the course of our working sessions I learnt that Pat hailed from Peterborough where the family operated the Embassy theatre. Remarkably for a woman at that time, Pat had amazingly wide experience of theatre business: she had held admin appointments in the world of ice shows, with Bertram Mills Circus at Olympia, and in the contracts department of Moss Empires before - after much travelling abroad - joining the Carl Rosa Opera Company and then being recruited by Arlen as his PA when he became involved with the National. With such a pedigree it was no wonder that her ability with figures and knowledge of the touring scene was fantastic.

I had some knowledge of the contemporary commercial theatre scene outside London from general theatre gossip but it was Pat who gave me the general picture as far as the provinces (as we called them then) were concerned. Two commercial circuits still controlled the majority of the large theatres visited by Sadler's Wells Opera and touring commercial productions: Moss Empires (to all intents and purposes the same company as the Coliseum's landlords, Stoll Theatres Corporation) and its rival, Howard and Wyndham. In cities such as Liverpool each company controlled a theatre and Sadler's Wells alternated to an extent between them though the Empire (Moss controlled) had an even larger capacity than the Coliseum so took some filling. Pat gave me the background as to how to assess which theatre to book whenever there was a choice. Birmingham had a family-run independent theatre, the Alexandra, and its director Derek Salberg had a strong family theatre background (his brother ran the subsidised Playhouse in Salisbury) whilst Moss operated the larger Hippodrome. There were cities with overlapping catchment areas such as Newcastle upon Tyne and Sunderland where local politics had to be taken into account. There were also very independent and isolated dates like Norwich where the Theatre Royal was managed by dedicated people concerned to get product for their venue from the national companies. It might be the repertoire which dictated the most suitable venue, or whose 'turn' it was when there was little to choose between rival theatres; all such considerations were carefully assessed by Pat. A few years later the Arts Council took on the role of deciding which companies toured where ('spheres of influence) but when I first became involved in tour planning it was the companies which made such decisions – and with just as much weighing up of pros and cons as the Arts Council would later do rather laboriously. In an odd way this was probably an Arlen legacy.

By the time I became involved in UK touring, commercial theatres had little capacity for promoting the shows presented other than by distributing leaflets and posting posters on sites around the locality; the numbers of leaflets and posters required being the 'requisition' which each theatre provided to the visiting company. The quantities gave a fair indication of the venue's promotional capacity! In my publicity days the flying visits made to such theatres made it quite clear that, with a few exceptions, they felt they had no direct involvement beyond arranging poster sites and putting leaflets out.

The National's early tour dates even with Sir heading a cast were by and large poorly attended and I suspect it was this and the struggle for opera audiences which led Arlen to propose with John Tooley of the ROH the idea that the national companies (Royal Ballet, Sadler's Wells Opera and the National Theatre) should plan visits which saw them follow one another and most importantly promote the occasion as a mini festival. Thus was born the Dramatic and Lyric Theatres Association (DALTA) which later extended into other areas such as joint programme advertising. Its first employee, David Gideon Thompson, had been the repertoire manager at the National but when he went off to work in television he was succeeded by Jack Phipps who became a legend for conceiving a variety of schemes some of which blossomed (Opera North) and some of which didn't (Upstart)…

But all this was in the future and meanwhile 1971 drew to a close with more notable events.

The appearance of Janet Baker with the company in *The Coronation of Poppea* was scheduled to begin with a gala performance in aid of the Sadler's Wells Opera Benevolent Fund. Little did members of the administration at my level realise how, behind the scenes, Janet Baker's appearance with the company had been fraught with difficulties with Mackerras apparently arranging private support for her enhanced fee.

For me the gala was a new experience as it entailed a special (platonic) relationship with Pauline Grant, the director of the Movement Group. Pauline had created this when the company came to the Coliseum in recognition of the evolution of modern opera staging, whereby drama was now just as important as singing. Traditionally, opera ballet dancers were there purely to perform any set-piece dances within operas. Under Pauline's Movement Group, the dancers – while still not singing – began to move in a trained fashion and blend with the chorus, creating more fluid staging and becoming an integral part of the production (such as in the fights in the tobacco factory for Carmen). The Movement Group was uniquely Pauline's creation and her direction showed her background as choreographer and director. No surprise that she went on to provide invaluable input to Peter Hall's productions at Glyndebourne.

Pauline gave the appearance of being rather timid and without strong will. Nothing could have been further from the truth; her appearance belied a steely determination - she was often aptly described as the 'iron butterfly'. It was her social connections - her address book - which Arlen turned to when faced with how best to get the gala wheels turning. Pauline was the widow of Sam Newsome who had run the Coventry Theatre and been a major car dealer in the Midlands. Pauline herself was a distinguished West End choreographer with many notable successes behind her. At Arlen's request she volunteered one of her close friends to chair the necessary Gala Committee. This was Dorothy, Lady Hulse (who delighted in being known as Dimpy!) - a great character, even if not a particularly organised lady.

Our early meetings were at the Hulse residence (a tiny period house off Park Lane) over lunch. The table always had a chair for her poodle to sit and observe what was eaten. It took a while to assemble really effective committee members; two early recruits, Graeme Tonge and Hans Wallach, became good friends – and stalwarts of all the gala committees throughout my time with the company. Graeme was a senior executive at Austin Reed (the clothing retailers) while Hans was a refugee from central Europe in the 30s who started the high class silk tie manufacturers, Michelsons. Between them they set about persuading many of their business colleagues to take programme advertisements which I came to realise was a major part of any gala fund raising activity. Many others from the social pages of Pauline's address book joined up and a respectable house was eventually sold.

My previous Sadler's Wells gala experience with Princess Margaret and the heart-stopping 'almost kiss' was certainly useful when setting up the FOH performance arrangements to look after the Queen Mother, who had accepted the chairman, David McKenna's invitation to grace the event. I was slightly surprised at Arlen's lack of involvement but as he had once made a comment about royals staying in their palaces I thought little of it until it became clear that he was, in fact, seriously ill and had to go to hospital and miss the performance itself. Those at my level had no idea just how serious his condition was but enjoyed seeing his young daughter present the obligatory bouquet in the foyer, collecting a press quote for her demand to her mother immediately she had done so, "Now can I have that ice cream?"

*The Queen Mother receiving a bouquet from Juliet Arlen before
attending the gala of The Coronation of Poppea Dec 1 1971*

In the early days of January 1972 we all had a tremendous
shock when Arlen died in hospital. He was someone with
connections back to early times of the opera company and
great knowledge of all aspects of theatre. Although often
demanding he was great fun to work for. The performance

at the Coliseum was cancelled the evening he died and John Tooley made a curtain speech expressing condolences at the Royal Opera House. What would the future hold for us all? At the time I remember it entailed much discussion of how to ensure the financial year did not end with a surplus brought about by Arlen's programme planning success – thereby prejudicing future Arts Council grants.

. . . .

Call me George

I had been aware of Lord Harewood's passion for music and opera in particular from general press comment around his tenure as the director of the Edinburgh Festival. I had also heard his name mentioned when Arlen talked about the Midland Opera scheme based on Wolverhampton's Grand Theatre and the use of Bingley Hall in Birmingham (what foresight in an odd way when you reflect on the later Opera North and the Birmingham concert hall). So it wasn't a great surprise when his name came forward as the new MD. There was of course an advertisement of the post (!) though Mackerras made it clear he considered it a foregone conclusion. Other directors of the company kept their counsel – though one declared that he could never work with 'that man' but changed his mind rather quickly.

I do not remember very much about the board meeting after Harewood was appointed as at that meeting I was appointed Company Secretary (I think at the instigation of the Finance Director, John Snape, perhaps not relishing minuting duties himself!). Thus began my career as a minute writer! I managed to produce some passable narrative of meetings whilst David McKenna was chairman but his successor, Kenneth Robinson, asked me to go to his office 'for coffee and a chat' after the first two or three of his meetings I minuted. Robinson, a health minister in Harold Wilson's first premiership, was erudite and very literate (writing a very readable biography of Wilkie Collins). Over coffee in his office at the British Steel Corporation (which overlooked Buckingham Palace grounds, prompting Harewood to remark on one visit that the flamingos were pinker than in the bird park at Harewood House), he implied that I was not producing minutes in the style he expected. He then gave some memorable advice with tongue only slightly in cheek: "Always remember that it is not a record of what was said, nor what someone thought they said, but rather what they would have said if they had thought about it". Robinson was always easy to serve and a great help to the company in his years in the chair before he moved on to chairing the Arts Council. He also served as Chair of London Transport after retiring from British Steel, claiming responsibility for instigating the decoration of the platforms at Charing Cross underground station. Robinson's comments on my minutes had their effect over the years prompting his successor as chairman Lord Goodman to suggest, in typical Goodman fashion, that if there was a vacancy for cabinet secretary he would support my candidature…

It was after a board meeting whilst those management who were in attendance were collecting papers together that Harewood requested 'can we drop the Lord Harewood, please' and so began 'call me George'. There was even a suggestion that in official literature and publicity he should be listed as George Harewood but that never got as far as print. In many ways Harewood made you forget his aristocratic background but there were the odd occasions – such as when he asked how much biscuits cost - when you realised he did little housekeeping himself.

Whilst the opera company had operated from Sadler's Wells Theatre it made many continental tours with the assistance of the British Council. Arlen had negotiated for the company to appear in Munich during the 1972 Olympics and Harewood headed the company for that engagement. The company achieved great acclaim with Britten's *Gloriana* and I received on behalf of the company a very simple settlement in ready deutschmarks (without the usual contra deductions, which was a pleasant surprise). It was somewhat daunting to be walking even a short way with a briefcase full of deutschmarks but no doubt such cash settlement was all part of financing the arts Olympics as far as the Munich authorities were concerned. Sadly, the return to Luton airport was marred by the news of the horrific massacre of Israeli athletes just after the company had left Munich.

Shortly before the trip to Munich I had been summoned by Harewood and invited to take on the role of Administrative Director. I was agreeably surprised and so carried away I didn't tell my close management colleagues before they saw the announcement …

As far as my work was concerned, I still had no formal job description but I was to a large extent involved with the Finance Director in the negotiations with stage staff. 1973 saw storm clouds gathering on the industrial relations front when the Royal Ballet visited, with the ROH management objecting to stage staff costs resulting from Coliseum shift patterns. It was at this time I got to know Guy Bloomer who, as Administrative Manager at the ROH, had the challenge of all union negotiations there. We found ourselves making frequent contact as the time passed. The Royal Ballet season passed peacefully as in the last resort the ROH paid up - they always seemed to find the necessary cash.

As well as the regular visit by London Festival Ballet that year we had the first visit by a company presented by the Hochhausers, Victor and Lilian, of Georgian State Dancers - except it wasn't because they gauged the general feelings about Russian/Soviet companies would mean their involvement would not go down well within their Jewish circles. Thus it was that we met Raymond Gubbay. Raymond had worked for the Hochhausers until he felt he had learnt enough and set up his own operation. It was his company which took over the Georgian presentation. It was most notable for me as I had arranged for them to use the new dance floor onstage which London Festival Ballet had laid for their preceding season. As the Georgians set about hurling their sabres around and into the floor I wondered about the comeback from LFB when they next used the floor. Fortunately, the scars of the sabre battle weren't noticed.

In October 1973 the opera company was invited to present *Gloriana* at the Europhalia Festival in Belgium. I had been able to secure the Australian Ballet to appear at the Coliseum while the company was abroad. By this time touring had become a major battle with regard to technical staff costs – what would the touring allowance be and how would the 'get out' be costed? The touring allowance for foreign tours was fixed by the British Council based on the cost of certain items, but the get out was another matter. This originated, as I understood it, in the days when at the end of a season at a theatre an extra group of casual labour would be engaged to get out scenery and effects as fast as possible and paid cash for doing so. By the '70s this was seen as the opportunity of collecting a bonus in addition to whatever wages (often including substantial overtime) were earned. Looking back it seems ridiculous that it was impossible to negotiate better arrangements but, despite many efforts with the technicians' union, NATTKE, this didn't happen. The particular crunch over the Europhalia tour is now (happily) forgotten, but after the battles over UK touring earlier in the year it was decided that the touring allowance demanded (over and above that fixed by the British Council) would not be met. The tour was cancelled. Europhalia became Eurofailure. Huisman, who was a major player on the Belgian side, was not happy.

. . . .

A significant name change

'Sadler's Wells Opera at the London Coliseum' was clearly not the best description for a company setting out to attract audiences, especially those who had no idea of its background at Islington. Arlen had hoped that the company could become the National Opera, complementing the international opera on offer at the Royal Opera House. However, such names are not easily acquired, as Harewood soon discovered. In partnership with chairman Kenneth Robinson, Harewood continued the quest for a new name which Arlen had started before his death. Apart from removing public confusion as to where exactly they would find the opera, St Martin's Lane or Rosebery Avenue, it was felt the company *deserved* a more appropriate name.

By 1973 the opera company had performed extensively on the Continent with British Council support and sent a company to Australia. But there was reluctance in official circles (and probably at the Royal Opera House) to have a National Opera. Gradually, after an appeal by Robinson using all his political skills with the government official responsible for 'sensitive names' (really!), the compromise of 'English' being added to the title emerged. The inevitable abbreviation to ENO was of great concern to Robinson's board members who only reluctantly accepted the new name. When the first pieces of print emerged in red and blue, one board member took great delight in presenting me with packets of ENO's

Fruit Salts – a popular brand of laxative at the time – which also had the letters in those colours on their packaging.

There was a certain amount of mileage to be had from the name change: in selling the 1973 tours we stressed that these would be the last performances by the company under its Sadler's Wells banner. The new 1974/5 season duly opened on August 3 with a revival of *La Traviata*, after a brief but telling name change campaign - without any mention of fruit salts.

• •

1974 Annus horribilis

The first days of 1974 saw me in Monte Carlo and then Copenhagen - the former at the invitation of the Tokyo Ballet via their European agent, Boris Trailine, the latter to finalise arrangements for the Royal Danish Ballet season at the Coliseum. These visits were part of my aim to ensure there was always a taker for any available weeks at the Coliseum (while the opera company was on tour or holiday) and so avoid the dark weeks of previous years with their disastrous effect on finances. Nothing came of the Japanese until they participated in a Nureyev Festival some years later, but the Danes successfully presented a short season in April at the Coli whilst the opera company was on tour giving their last performances as Sadler's Wells Opera.

During the early months of the year pressure was on to finalise the visit of the Bolshoi Ballet to the Coliseum.

A season had been planned in '73 but never actually confirmed. (Such a season had been on the agenda with the Hochhausers back in Arlen's time, perhaps as part of his slightly wicked way of getting one step ahead of the ROH where the Hochhausers had presented dance seasons for many years.) The international political situation had not improved since the Georgians' visit, being exacerbated by the Russian refusal to grant visas for Jewish artists wishing to emigrate to Israel. The Bolshoi visit was on/off for much of the spring before the Russian state agency, Gosconcert, confirmed the trip and we got the go ahead to open booking. This saw the box office swamped in much the same way as that at the Old Vic had been in the early National days - but things eventually calmed down for the simple reason of being sold out for most of the six week season.

The political situation, however, did not calm down and pressure mounted on the Hochhausers to cancel the visit or withdraw from its management. A major campaign had developed around the refusal to allow two Kirov dancers, the Panovs (Valery and Galina), to emigrate from the USSR to Israel. Permission was finally given during the London Festival Ballet season at the Coliseum prior to the Bolshoi, but this did nothing to reduce passions. As far as we were concerned we had to maintain the booking if for no other reason than the rent which was at stake. Harewood was put in a difficult PR position but with board backing remained committed. Despite vociferous protest – much reported in the press - and physical demonstrations as the company arrived in London, the six week season eventually opened on June 12. The Times 'Jon' cartoon the following day neatly summed things up showing a dancer on stage accompanied with burly police officers and two front row audience members remarking 'security is damned tight here tonight'.

Thus began what became an exhausting time of protests by a series of pro-Jewish organisations (interspersed with a few known trouble makers cashing in on the act, the police reckoned). Protests took every form imaginable – umbrellas with slogans being opened in the auditorium, mice released in the stalls and, worst of all, tacks being thrown on stage. Whilst the tacks were the most dangerous, the release of white mice caused the most havoc. I was alerted by staff about mice being reported by audience members and had to get all available staff to creep around grabbing all the mice they could while the performance continued. A few mice were put in an empty ice bucket and these were shown to David English of The Daily Mail who had been in that evening's audience and initially complained of the disruption around his seat but came round after seeing the culprits! After the tacks were thrown, I had to make an announcement from the stage about the performance being halted while 'dangerous objects are removed'. This was recorded by the ballet critic of The Times, John Percival, in not very complimentary terms ("some white-coated individual berated the audience…") but was later the subject of much amusement when we lunched together and he heard the whole story.

In addition to all these incidents, we also had to deal with the company's Russian administration or, more accurately, their KGB minders, a succession of whom appeared, none of whom were terribly communicative. There were, however, some relaxing social (and PR-friendly) moments such as when we took the company off to Windsor Safari Park (pre-Legoland days) where a baby lion was named Leo by one of the company's principals, Tatiana Bessmertnova. As the six week season drew to a close we began to relax and by the penultimate night were almost euphoric. Two events, however, made the last part of the season memorable for all the wrong reasons.

*A rare peaceful Bolshoi moment: naming
a lion cub at Windsor Safari Park*

Along the sides of the Coliseum were properties which Oswald Stoll had been unable to acquire when assembling the site for his new theatre. Immediately adjacent to the theatre in St Martin's Lane up a tiny passageway was an old warehouse. In the late evening of July 19 a fire began there. The first we knew about it was when firemen appeared in the back of the Circle having somehow entered via an emergency exit. Thankfully the performance was drawing to its close and the audience left without too much confusion. The theatre itself was undamaged – but it was a disconcerting experience.

The final curtain call of the six week Bolshoi season 1974

Further, that same night saw the Turkish invasion of Cyprus. The Russians, already unsettled by the weeks of protest, were convinced there was some international conspiracy afoot. It was something of a miracle that the two performances took place the following Saturday. Thankfully, they passed without further incident and the final curtain calls for *Spartacus* saw the stage inundated with flowers and the company obviously greatly moved by their reception.

Unfortunately, the following day again saw protesters outside the company's hotel in Whitehall, providing a less-than-ideal departure from a memorable tour. Sue and I recharged our batteries with our first visit to Corsica a few days later.

1974 had already been a memorable year: Edward Heath had used emergency powers to declare a three day week in January as part of his battle with the Miners' Union, then called and lost an election in February which resulted in Harold Wilson's return to Downing Street with Michael Foot as Employment Secretary acceding to the miners' demands. Inflation hit 20%. This was the context for an unhappy chapter of industrial relations for the new English National Opera, all in the year marking the centenary of the birth of Lilian Baylis who had founded both the national opera and ballet companies.

As a result of earlier industrial difficulties like the Europhalia cancellation and touring allowance disputes, Robinson had brought in Gerald Wood of management consultants Urwick Orr and Partners as a personnel advisor. Technically the appointment was by Harewood and part of a wider industrial relations consultancy but as, one later learned, there was 'history'. Urwick Orr had apparently been involved in a review of Edinburgh Festival administration during the Harewood regime which had not been that successful. After Arlen's death the finance director, John Snape, had headed negotiations with NATTKE, but after my appointment as Administrative Director this poisoned chalice came my way and I worked closely with Wood. Whilst one couldn't fault his analytical approach he sometimes lacked urgency which I should probably have challenged.

I have already alluded to the unsatisfactory stage work patterns which came about with the move to the Coliseum. As the 74/5 season got under way with *La Traviata* a dispute arose about the shift pattern and pay in the running wardrobe. This resulted in strike action for several days in August until a new pattern and increased pay were agreed. It had been intended that with Wood's help, we (myself and Snape) would consider and then negotiate the proposals which the stage staff negotiating committee had agreed to put forward for better working arrangements and to effect economies, all within the prevailing 'pay code'. However, this never happened and the committee was replaced by a more active (militant, I am inclined to say and 'hot headed' according to one of the crew at the time) bunch.

By the time *The Bassarids* (with composer Hans Werner Henze much involved) had opened there was considerable hostility, not helped by the poor management of NATTKE's local officer. Although I was considered to be the real villain for failing to meet or negotiate, my brief was clearly set out by the board and guided by Wood. On October 31 the stage staff decided to work to rule (disastrous for the running of *The Bassarids* with various scene changes in public view). The actual sequence of events was hotly disputed and I am not even sure that the subsequent Committee of Enquiry satisfactorily established what happened - but that evening's performance came to a halt when staff failed to carry out scheduled tasks. Then, with Wood's guidance, Harewood's express approval and after consultation with Robinson and a special board meeting, 46 stage staff were dismissed. At first 'unofficial' but later declared official by NATTKE, the resulting strike saw 32 performances cancelled until finally both sides agreed to a SWETM/NATTKE conciliation board.

SWETM (Society of West End Theatre Management) was the management body representing theatre managements in London's West End. Although subsidised theatre - drama and lyric - was represented in membership (which was personal), it was more tolerated than welcomed. Indeed, when Arlen had written to the Society's Secretary at the time of the move to the Coliseum about more active membership the answer was somewhat dusty. Strange, given Arlen's record in commercial management and relationship with Prince Littler, one of the West End's senior players. I had become a member in 1972 by virtue of my role but hadn't played any part in Society business apart from attendance at occasional meetings. Consequently, when it came to the conciliation board I was an unknown quantity and Wood, who presented management's case, was viewed with great suspicion being from the 'consultancy' world. The board's findings were very critical of labour relations at the Coliseum and declared that dismissing 46 staff had been contrary to 'natural justice'.

All this went down very badly with us. Despite a lot of discussion about challenging the legality of the board's actions, performances were resumed on December 17, after - with Lord Goodman's involvement - it had been agreed the Arts Council would convene a Committee of Enquiry. Lord Goodman had by now become the natural person to consult when a problem arose in a variety of fields. (Heath had sent him to try and sort things out in Rhodesia with Ian Smith, he had chaired an inquiry into the future of opera with Harewood, and sat on various arts boards, so was widely respected as a 'fixer'). The Enquiry was duly set up and, when it reported well into '75, rejected the conciliation board's view that management was 'solely to blame for bad industrial relations' and pointed to the 15 hour day shift pattern of work over three days in the working week as a major part of the problem.

My own view of management members on the SWETM conciliation board was that they had perhaps given undue weight to the fact that performances of *Peter Pan* being mounted by a commercial manager (Tom Arnold Ltd now headed by Arnold's widow Helen and son Tom who actually won a Tory seat in 1974) might have been cancelled with significant loss of revenue. The show, as it were, must go on. I also reckoned that I should have given more attention to befriending the West End! There were repercussions within the Society as a result of criticism of its behaviour: a specific committee was formed comprising representatives of the subsidised and commercial managements to monitor union agreements in both areas. I had attempted to do this throughout the strike and there were frequent meetings with Guy Bloomer from the Opera House, Simon Relph from the National and occasionally David Brierley from the RSC which the Society's Secretary, Bob Lacy Thomson, attended. I am not sure how much any report he might have made was heeded.

By this time our technical director had already resigned and a personal friend, Peter Bentley Stephens, who had been Stage Controller and directly involved in the October 31 events was made redundant. A good thing for me was the decision to recruit an outsider (James Sargeant) to take control of stage affairs from now on. Stage staff eventually settled into a new working pattern perhaps as a result of many militants moving on to plague Peter Hall as the new National Theatre attempted to get under way on the South Bank (though there was a near strike early in '75 – and a real strike up the road at the Hippodrome/Talk of the Town).

The year had also brought personal grief – in the midst of the strike my father had died after two years of poor health following a major operation. How Sue and I wanted a new year.

· ·

Changed Priorities

I think at one stage after the strike I thought of leaving ENO but reckoned there was a lot I could still achieve; after John Snape, the Finance Director, also left I set about ensuring my areas ran like clockwork. Another consideration was that we were expecting our first child in mid 1975. Sue had by now established a busy design practice and numbered among her clients many of the managements which brought shows to the Coliseum. She decided to give up the work she undertook for the opera company but continued with other theatre companies.

After the Bolshoi any foreign company would have been a contrast but the Hochhausers certainly came up with a sharp one: this was a two week visit by a Chinese martial arts company! That summer saw the opera company giving a guest performance of *Gloriana* at the Volksoper in Vienna and *Patience* at the Theater an der Wien. I was not directly involved in the tour, concentrating instead on very domestic matters – our daughter arrived at the end of July in the midst of a terrific heatwave. We had just about finished work on our first house in Clapham but one thing we struggled with was to find a name for our newcomer; it was my assistant Richard Jarman who suggested 'Tamasin' one morning, probably to get a decision out of me on another pressing matter. Richard made a great success of managing the visit to Vienna, which stood him in good stead for later work as John Drummond's assistant at the Edinburgh Festival. He later rescued Scottish Opera at a difficult time and guided London Festival Ballet to become English National Ballet, not forgetting the final phase of the Royal Opera House's reopening after its major restoration.

Property management had always interested me and been a major part of my work 'portfolio' but by 1975 attention was focussed on the approaching end date of the company's ten year lease in 1978. As part of this we had consulted with Lord Goodman (of course) who had introduced us to the property management company and agents, George Trollope & Sons. As a result we had the good fortune to acquire the expertise of one of the directors, Ian Glover, who until his early death a short while later gave invaluable advice and helped us initiate planned maintenance. It would still be a battle to protect maintenance expenditure in the budget but at least there was now some professional input.

By now Lord Grade was the boss of our landlord's company, Stoll Theatres Corporation, and the matter of a new lease led to an early morning encounter with him in his vast office at ATV. No one at that time thought of anywhere other than the Coliseum as the company's base, so it was certainly a shock when Grade with his architect Richard Seiffert at his elbow came out with the proposal that ENO should move to the Theatre Royal Drury Lane. At this time (pre-Mackintosh/Lloyd Webber hits) it wasn't always easy to find shows for such a big house and Grade reckoned the opera could use the space at the Lane while he developed part of the stage at the Coliseum for another Seiffert tower, a regular feature of Seiffert developments – his Centre Point was widely reviled for its intrusion into the West End landscape. There followed a series of secretive visits by a small group of ENO senior personnel to the Lane before the message 'no thank you' went back to Grade. Whilst there was undoubtedly more space backstage and front of house at the Lane we were all wary of its location around the corner from the Royal Opera House and tucked away from Trafalgar Square. An extension of the Coliseum lease for another ten year period followed and we heard no more of the relocation idea.

With a more secure tenancy we were able to reassess our needs in St Martin's Lane. At the time of the move to the Coliseum it had not been possible to repossess all of the building from the tenancies Stoll Theatres had created in their bid to find revenue in the days when the theatre had been used for cinema. At the time of the move to the Coliseum, Arlen had persuaded Prince Littler to end the tenancy on

'Century House' – an office unit which had been created out of several original dressing rooms and the one sizeable room backstage. This had become an opera rehearsal room, of sorts. We had also leased various small properties around the Coliseum resulting in a rather disjointed property portfolio, even including a warehouse space in Shelton Street, Covent Garden, acquired when the famous market had relocated to Nine Elms. This provided prop storage and a workshop – the latter had been tucked away high up in the flys backstage until the authorities had rightly condemned it. Where could we find space to improve backstage conditions?

When I made the building tour with the surveyor who had already helped with small building projects, it was the area under the stage housing the revolve machinery which caught his interest. It was felt this was the only space left for some kind of development. After considerable discussion - perhaps wrangling is a better word - at many levels, a brief was agreed: a proper band room, dressing rooms for the Movement Group (Pauline Grant's versatile dancers) and a full-time canteen to replace a makeshift operation backstage during performances and the use of a front-of-house buffet during non public times. All to be achieved without the loss of performances by night working! Incredibly this was achieved and these spaces still function as intended. Of course, using space under stage meant restricting space for use as stage traps and inevitably the area originally reserved for technical use had to be extended but we did thankfully achieve more SPACE...

Another major property upheaval came when the company's rehearsal studios and making wardrobe in Aldgate, Camperdown House, were redeveloped. These were located in what I believe was originally a boys' club and then the rehearsal centre for the very successful commercial theatre impresario, Harold Fielding. The lease had been acquired when the company was at Rosebery Avenue and the building continued to provide vital facilities after the move to the Coliseum. It also housed the Motley Design Course in the sizeable but uninviting basement. This had also originated at Rosebery Avenue (in the house next door to the theatre in a kind of 'loose' council tenancy arrangement, the type of which Arlen was adept at arranging). Quite a hive of mixed activity!

Camperdown House was a property in the portfolio of a member of the Wingate family. In 1980 he decided the time was ripe for a redevelopment and instead of allowing us to negotiate a lease extension we were faced with an (admittedly valid) notice to quit. There was obviously much at stake as far as the development was concerned because it was put to us that early vacation (in terms of months, I think) would come with a financial incentive. At this time we were fortunate in having more help from Trollopes: a skilled property negotiator, James Owen, checked the proposal and urged acceptance. The Whitechapel Art Gallery was also involved in the redevelopment and I remember a phone call from Nicholas Serota (then the director at the Gallery) who obviously also had some incentive to assist Wingate's plans, assuring us that the scheme was genuine. (Ironically, it was Serota as chair of the Arts Council who proposed that ENO should leave London in 2022.)

The search for new rehearsal spaces was on. I visited a number of redundant churches – they certainly had space to meet the rehearsal room part of the brief – and a great variety of other structures. It was a new experience for me to come across large properties standing idle in the capital. Finally the former Decca Recording Studios in West Hampstead appeared on the list to inspect. Here at last was a building which could provide a good size rehearsal room (even if not exactly replicating the Coliseum stage), ancillary practice rooms and sufficient space for the making wardrobe. It had been agreed that the design course could no longer be supported and Margaret Harris had already set about her own property search. When I enthusiastically reported back to my colleagues not everyone was happy (no change there) but finally it was agreed that the building could be made to work as a replacement for Camperdown House. There followed a mad scramble. The legalities were no great problem (thank you Goodman Derrick) but arranging a completely clear Camperdown House to comply with the deal for the cash bonus proved a challenge until, after much screaming, this was achieved and the cash bonus came our way. The building was renamed Lilian Baylis House and in due course 'opened' by our patron, Princess Alexandra.

*Greeting ENO's patron, Princess
Alexandra, at Lilian Baylis House*

I can no longer remember the exact figures involved
in this exercise (missing that little notebook!) but I believe
the new premises cost around £800k, a large proportion of
which came from the Wingate cash early vacation bonus,
the rest from the Arts Council who understandably then
had a stake in the property. It amuses me to read now in
an official company history ['Opera for Everybody'] that
the purchase of the Decca Studios was all about reducing
overheads with no mention of our major property deal,
which resulted in the company actually owning real
estate for the first time! Did I write those board minutes so
inaccurately? It is one of many occasions where I reflect on
my words providing the company's history.

Some account of Harewood's management style is appropriate to explain how matters such as these property affairs were conducted. Harewood was the company's chief executive as Managing Director. Major billing was also given to the music directors and, in later years, production directors on all publicity.The senior management team comprised the directors of finance, drama and text, opera planning and technical areas besides administration. Development came later and will certainly appear in this narrative. These directors comprised the directorate, which in Harewood's time met roughly every other week over lunch. The agenda comprised any urgent items a director wanted to get colleagues' views on as well as more general items. Harewood was always willing to have general discussion on issues which any director put forward at one of these meetings but made it clear whose was the final word! Artistic matters were only really on the agenda in the context of costs; the board had an opera committee where artistic plans were hammered out. Bernard Williams (Provost of King's College, Cambridge) and Leopold de Rothschild apparently sometimes took issue with Harewood's plans but as I did not attend those meetings I only heard what was reported at board meetings. Whilst I never felt Harewood had the natural grasp of finance which had been the case with Arlen, he could present a good case with figures if they were clearly presented to him. Snape's successor as finance director, Caroline Phillips, was good at the presentation but her approach sometimes irritated Harewood. On the whole this directorate worked well and the only major plan which caused trouble with the board was the American Tour of 1985.

Harewood's relations with the board were interesting. Some board members were particularly deferential to Harewood but most took their responsibilities very seriously as you would expect from the likes of ex cabinet ministers Robert Carr and Edmund Dell. I think we were very lucky with our board members. Their selection would of course now be seen as very incorrect: the board identified possible candidates for membership but had no established criteria for election. Rotation was laid down in the Articles and most members served no more than two terms.

After the 1974 strike the GLC, as a major funder, took more interest in nominating their member (probably because Tony Banks, though technically a member at the time, had failed to keep them fully informed of developments, having only attended, I think, one meeting). The new GLC nominee, Paul Boateng, was a breath of fresh air. Goodman surprised everyone by recruiting Edmund Dell the weekend he resigned from the government and inviting him to a board meeting the following Monday! Of course this raised a few eyebrows but given the prospect of such a catch no one raised any objection. Dell became the chairman of the board's finance committee where he was not averse to asking searching questions of management.

Another member who made considerable efforts to help the company outside actual meetings was Colin Wills, whose family had many television and sporting venue interests, Wembley Stadium being one. Wills tried to exploit the BBC's decision to allow producers freedom in their choice of production company rather than always having to produce programmes in-house at the BBC. He also used his contacts to set up a number of meetings where the idea of topping and tailing a TV programme might finance an opera transmission – now very familiar in commercial television as "XYZ company sponsors late night television". His own ability as a producer was apparent at the wonderful black and gold party he gave to celebrate his 50th birthday – top of the bill in the cabaret was the Beverley Sisters.

Two important people in my career, Kenneth Rae (left) and Lord Goodman (right)

Lord Goodman featured in many of the company's affairs during my time, particularly its crises, but his most significant contribution was as its chairman, a role he took on in 1978 when Kenneth Robinson was appointed chairman of the Arts Council. Unlike Robinson, Goodman was not one for detailed study of board papers, much to Harewood's exasperation. After many difficult moments at a meeting when it became clear that Goodman had not read all his papers (prompting much harumphing – which we referred to as the Hanoverian cough! - and finger drumming from Harewood) we took to providing very detailed notes, almost a script! As Harewood spent most weekends at home in Yorkshire (unless there was an important Saturday performance) and board meetings were lunchtime on a Monday, it meant that if the train was late it was difficult for senior management to get together with him for a proper briefing to rehearse the 'party line' before facing the full board. On the Monday after the weekend news had featured Harewood's first wife (Marion Stein) marrying Jeremy Thorpe, there was the innocent comment from Harewood about Marion never making a good choice in men... There were also occasions when you were reminded of Harewood's illustrious family (he being the Queen's cousin and sharing the royal family's lineage, hence the Hanoverian references). When the Duke of Windsor's funeral clashed with some formal meeting, it wasn't clear until the last moment that he was not on the guest list (instead, he wore a black tie with a Windsor knot for the day).

In later years the board held an annual retreat which, it has to be admitted, came about after the ROH board had established the practice. The first retreat was held under Goodman's auspices as Master at University College,

Oxford. I found it challenging but enjoyable preparing the papers for the discussions. Harewood asked me to arrange the programme so that the board had a session without any of us employees present. When I presented the draft to Goodman he protested that he couldn't imagine what the board would talk about without us present! – but they no doubt spent the time agonising over the US tour, a hot topic at the time. The retreat started with an evening meal on the Friday and Harewood was not slow to comment on the host's wine cellar – as Goodman was teetotal University College probably took little care in wine selection for the Master's cellar, concentrating on the tastes of the rest of the high table. Post dinner relaxation gave rise to interesting stories from members; one from Bernard Williams stayed with me about a session of Cambridge dons discussing what size an angel on a memorial should be. 'Half life-size' had been the decision by the well-dined group.

. . . .

Extra Curricular Activity and how!

I kept in touch with Raymond Mander and Joe Mitchenson for both professional and personal reasons – they were invaluable for answering odd questions about the Coliseum's history as well as being regular suppliers to Sue of material for programme design. They were also great characters to have as friends. However, by the mid-70s their Collection had reached a crisis.

*Raymond Mander (left) and Joe Mitchenson (right)
proudly displaying a Noël Coward dressing gown at
Venner Road, the original home of their collection*

From the earliest days of the National's planning for the new South Bank complex, it had been envisaged that their Collection would have a home in the new theatre. However, as time passed I learnt from careful asides from Yolande Bird and the 'boys' themselves that this wasn't going to happen. In many ways it would have been a waste of valuable space and there were surely better ways of securing the Collection's future (it being *our passport to posterity*' as Sybil Thorndike famously put it). Ray and Joe decided to hand over the Collection to a charitable trust in 1977 when it became clear that there was no future home on offer on the South Bank and I was delighted to be invited to be one of their first trustees. This was something of a two edged sword since Ray and Joe expected to go on running things as they always had done and their solicitor, Bill Fournier, who became the trust's first chairman, wasn't keen or able to alter their ways.

This was all very well until their house at Sydenham was threatened by a road widening scheme which brought an outcry from the theatre world. The local authority, Lewisham, then had a change of heart and offered the Collection a Georgian property in their care, Beckenham Place Park. An impressive building but not ideally suited for museum purposes (though better than its then use as changing rooms for the local golfers). I think it has now reverted to something of a community centre as both our children have made visits there for parties and the like.

The Lewisham offer of the Beckenham mansion started a fundraising campaign with some commitment (pangs of conscience?) from one or two National Board members, goaded I felt sure by Yolande. Sadly, Ray died in 1985 but Joe remained active for some while, eventually moving with the Collection into the mansion even though there was no formal lease! All a little unsatisfactory and I suppose I should have voiced more concern to Bill than I did. Fundraising benefited from the patronage of Olivier who accepted on the proviso he would write no more than one letter a year as he was completing his autobiography! There were some very successful fundraising lunches at the Whitbread Brewery in the City (organised by a great husband and wife team Harold and Mary Bonnett) which featured a theatre personality hosting a table for those prepared to pay for the privilege. Bill Fournier was legal adviser to Trevor Nunn and used this connection to secure a donation from Cameron Mackintosh, now flush with the success of *Cats*. Unfortunately, Bill didn't tie up the paperwork as well as he might have done and when Lewisham decided for financial reasons that the work on the mansion and the lease to the Collection could not, in fact, go ahead Cameron decided, not unreasonably, that the money should be returned. Sadly, Bill died before all this and, as I had succeeded him as chairman, I was left with a difficult negotiation with Cameron and the Charity Commissioners. Things were eventually resolved by the return of Cameron's gift and a telling off from the Charity Commissioners, things not being exactly helped by Tony Field (as one of our trustees) refusing to discuss the 'gift' with Cameron because of his close connection with him from Arts Council days.

By this time we had an impressive selection of trustees (Eddie Kulukundis, Tim and Pru West and Iain Mackintosh from the theatre world, Colin Ford - who had established the National Museum of Film Photography and Television at Bradford - and Danny La Rue, a long time friend of Ray and Joe. We also benefitted from the input of Henry McGee (most famous as Benny Hill's straight man) and Mary Jane Walsh with invaluable knowledge of educational fields. I had recruited as the Collection's full time Administrator Richard Mangan, a former very efficient Stage Manager at the National and subsequently with Michael Codron, as well as a popular lecturer on theatre in the States. So even though the threat of homelessness still loomed we seemed to be well equipped to look for new premises. One of my final actions for the Collection was to write the DNB entry for Ray and Joe, which entailed persuading the publishers that it should be a joint entry!

It is probably best (if not chronological) to include a note here about the subsequent history of the Collection. After the departure from Beckenham there was a brief period in a former Salvation Army premises before a move to what I hoped might be its permanent home at the Greenwich Naval College hosted by Gavin Henderson when he relocated Trinity College of Music there in great style in 2001. After my retirement the cost of staying at Greenwich became unsustainable - reproduction fees had declined significantly thanks to modern technology - so the Collection had to move again, this time to Bristol University

Theatre Collection. A brilliant organisation, but I doubt very much if Ray and Joe would consider it an ideal location for something so London-centric.

My work on M&M matters was largely in my own 'free' time but over the years I did find myself involved with some other projects. A couple for the Arts Council (performed in company time and therefore by negotiation with Harewood) even brought fees. The most dramatic was in connection with the management of the Aldeburgh Festival in October 1982.

This came about as a result of a chance meeting in St Martin's Lane with the Arts Council's music director, Basil Deane, who asked if I was free over a coming weekend to sit in on a discussion about management at Aldeburgh where Jack Phipps had taken over following his move from Arts Council touring. This seemed innocent enough and I agreed; I should have known better. On the face of it Phipps had been recruited to revive the Festival and all events at the Maltings following the death of Benjamin Britten, the founding father. According to Phipps he had been given a clear brief by the Chairman to expand and popularise the festival. Unfortunately, the Chairman died and his colleagues took fright at the way figures were going. It was hoped that with the input of some 'experts' knowledgeable in the field, Phipps' enthusiasm could be retained but expenses reduced. It quickly became clear that the locals on the governing body had little practical experience and were alarmed at how the deficit had more than doubled under

Phipps. He was always one for taking risks but his plans did, I recall, require some enormous leaps of faith in audience growth. It was one of the most harrowing weekends I had known trying to explain how the arts world worked to this group. I failed and Phipps resigned, eventually returning to the Arts Council, to be replaced by Kenneth Baird who had worked for me as house manager at the Coliseum. Not sure I logged this up as a great experience.

By contrast, work I did for the Arts Council on how theatre was structured in the North East and the Midlands was light relief!

. . . .

Nureyev and the dance world

After the Chinese martial arts company Lilian and Victor Hochhauser came up with a proposal for a Nureyev Festival. This would entail Rudolf Nureyev dancing at every performance with a company he had created a work specially for, or with whom he had already worked in some significant way. The first 'festival' in 1976 created a mad rush at the box office and was a sell-out success. As I had negotiated with Victor (and Lilian - they always made joint decisions) a good rent for the season and as all stage staff costs were picked up by the visiting management (unlike many West End contracts) the formula was good for all parties, so much so that eight seasons followed. By then Nureyev was no longer at his best (his performances on some occasions unkindly being described as 'near enough'). Amongst the companies participating was the Tokyo Ballet bringing memories of Monte Carlo! The festivals were certainly hard work but it was rewarding to be working with such dedicated professionals as Victor and Lilian with their careful attention to every bit of expenditure!

Nureyev performances attracted varied audiences so I was not surprised one day to get a message that Lady Albery was asking to buy house seats (ie some the management kept in reserve). On returning the call, I expected to be talking to Bronson Albery's widow but found instead I was put through to (his son) Donald Albery's wife, Nobuko, which was a shock as I had never spoken to her before and Donald was certainly not an admirer of our work at the Coliseum, his own son, Ian, having been one of the members of the infamous conciliation board in 1974. Nobuko launched straight into the reason for her call: gangway tickets for that evening's performance to accommodate Donald's stiff leg. Apparently Donald himself wouldn't dream of calling me! That visit broke the ice with the Alberys and we became quite friendly. Indeed when Donald retired my note wishing him well had a warm response with quite embarrassing detail of the arrangements made for Ian in the future management of the theatres. (They were sold to United Newspapers and much of Donald's 'archive' sold to an American university). It also led to acquaintance with an incredible Japanese lady balletomane, Masako Ohya, who was a close friend of Nobuko.

*Lord Harewood (left), Mrs Ohya and self
after his first meeting with her*

Madame Ohya decided that she would add dance at the
Coliseum to her itinerary whenever she could when visiting
England. This she seemed to do every year. On early visits
she was accompanied by her considerably older husband and
when on a later occasion they met Harewood he recalled
that Mr Ohya had stayed at the Harewood London residence
when on an official visit to London before WWII as part of
the entourage of the crown prince. It goes without saying
that the Ohyas were rich (at one stage owning Mikimoto
pearls) and after her husband died Madame Ohya set up
a foundation supporting her two great passions, golf and
ballet. Any visit to the Coliseum turned into a major event
– a greeting in the foyer, interval drinks (although we
invariably found her a private space, the refreshment was

always hot water and lemon) and umpteen photographs of course (copies of which subsequently came through the post and later featured in her foundation's publications!) She invariably went backstage to see Nureyev and it is probably as well that neither was conversant with the other's language as Nureyev didn't exude hospitality.

After a number of visits I suggested to Harewood that he should meet this character which led to an hilarious lunch with the Harewoods and Sue and myself, hosted by Madame Ohya in one of the restaurants she owned in London. Sue and I were also invited to the opening of her fish restaurant in St Christopher's Place but the combination of raw fish and Sue being pregnant didn't make for an enjoyable occasion. Later our appeals director, John Guy, became involved in the Ohya visits but we never achieved any substantial donation. I have however a collection of incredible Ohya photographs – some with her in unbelievable outfits for golf and ballet!

Nureyev's agent was Sandor Gorlinsky who, with his wife Edith, attended most Nureyev performances but somehow remained distant when Nureyev announced on certain occasions that the curtain would have to be delayed. The evening performance on a Saturday was often a nightmare as Nureyev was quite likely to demand the curtain up be delayed from 7.30 to 8.00. As it was impossible to contact the Hochhausers on a Saturday until sunset and Gorlinsky declined to be involved in such mundane matters, the only reassurance one had that the show would eventually go on was that Nureyev would get no fee if he didn't appear! Mind you that didn't stop him opting out of certain pieces in triple bills in the later seasons. I decided at an early stage in the first festival that I needed to remain at the theatre for much of each performance, especially on Saturdays. I am afraid that when Tamasin and then Darren were at an age to come to the theatre they were subjected to quite a lot of ballet matinees whilst Sue either worked or caught up at home with having worked late nights – not sure it did anything to encourage their interest in any form of dance! Being at the theatre during performance , however, led to many a long conversation with Victor and Sandor with revealing accounts of their early lives as impresarios in the immediate post WWII period.

A gathering of various theatre personalities in my office during an interval of a Nureyev performance – Sir Donald Albery, seated on floor second from left, Victor and Lilian Hochhauser back row second and third from right

The Hochhausers were not great believers in lavish entertainment but marked important events with generous hospitality. One of these after a Nureyev performance celebrated his birthday and gathered round the table was a galaxy of talent. Besides Nureyev himself and the Hochhausers, there was Rostropovitch (who spent much time in the Hochhauser office flat when first in the West), the critic (and friend of Nureyev's) Nigel Gosling and his wife, the former ballerina, Maude Lloyd (who provided a place for Nureyev to retreat to after matinees and before an evening show). Sue and I were definitely the 'others' around the table.

The Nureyev Festival was only part of the programme during the summer weeks between opera seasons. London Festival Ballet appeared regularly; indeed, as already mentioned, their involvement had been part of Coliseum planning from the start. The company always seemed to be able to pin their seasons on an anniversary which would then become a royal gala. There was something about galas involving dance that brought out the worst in their supporters with their management always demanding that little bit extra from us as the host management. The line up in the foyer for greeting the royal VIP was always lengthy and until I started demanding an ENO presence you would have thought LFB actually owned the building. The director who made a real effort to work with ENO was John Field who gelled more with Harewood than his predecessor Beryl Grey ever did, leading to performances of a Bartok double bill involving LFB and ENO. The Arts Council dance director often pushed us to allocate more weeks to LFB but then queried the high rent being quoted, which was based on what we could secure for a Nureyev season!

There was one person who was The Expert at making something special whenever there was a gala: Belle Shenkman, a rich Canadian resident in London. I first encountered her when the National Ballet of Canada came to the Coliseum in 1975 and she made practically every Canadian in London aware of the fact and signed up to support in some way. Her most memorable feat was transforming the front of house areas into a forest in full blossom for the gala attended by Princess Anne. The Canadian company made further visits and each time there was a transformation of the theatre, one memorable occasion featuring a brilliant display of vegetables by the florist Keith Turner - all done to 'dress the house' and provide a talking point, which it certainly did.

Before each season Belle invited the principals and administrative staff to an 'at home' at her flat overlooking the Royal Albert Hall. The address itself makes it clear that the flat was spacious. It was full of native Canadian sculptures which later were given a fitting showing at Canada House. I never discovered much about Belle's background other than meeting a charming daughter, but her husband, Desmond Blaise Smith was normally around. Many years later I was astounded to read in his obituary of his distinguished military career as a senior figure in the

Canadian army in the Normandy landings. Belle always operated simply as Belle Shenkman rather than using her married name of Shenkman Smith. I have never met anyone who exuded such style.

. . . .

More about catering

When I had arrived at the Coliseum catering had been run by a long-serving member of staff, Gertie Crocker, who had originally worked as secretary for Sam Harbour, a well-respected General Manager for much of the 50s. Sadler's Wells style catering with its array of cold meats and salads was a real challenge to Gertie in her advanced years, and in my early years as General Manager we decided to contract out to Westbys, a firm operating in many West End theatres. That also proved problematic (particularly for staff catering) and we turned to Gardner Merchant, (part of Trust House Forte) then with a high reputation for staff catering in particular. The real success of the contract was that they installed as the on-site manager, Heinz Keiffer. Heinz, originally from the German part of Switzerland, thrived at the Coliseum and, whilst faced with – and overcoming - many staff catering problems, managed to establish a very good reputation for public catering. He had many triumphs dealing with galas and special functions, particularly when some display was called for and he could demonstrate his skill in butter carving.

· ·

The thorny issue of touring

Goodman's arrival as chairman coincided with the problem of how best for the company to meet its touring obligations coming to a head. For some years the touring after the London season by a large and small company had seen declining audiences and poor financial return - so much so that the Arts Council's director of touring, Jack Phipps, had come up with a radical idea: the establishment of a separate company outside London specifically to tour. Where better to base this than in Yorkshire with its strong musical traditions, and where better in Yorkshire than the Grand Theatre Leeds?

I am not sure when exactly Jack Phipps came up with this plan, but there had been strong feelings in the regions for some time about having to put up with, as some saw it, second best – which was rarely, in fact, the case. The problem was that productions designed to fill the capacious Coliseum often had to be severely adapted to fit theatres outside London. Even if smaller productions went to smaller theatres on the 'weekly' tour the sets often suffered and lavish Lazaridis costumes might look wonderful on stage but made for cramped conditions in dressing rooms or blocked corridors presenting safety issues. There was also the problem of the poor state of repair of many regional theatres. Those which were commercially run (mostly by Stoll Moss) were much in need of renovation and lacked proper facilities for the touring company. (They also lacked any local publicity effort but change was to come later.)

Matters came to a head when Equity backed the opera chorus's blacklisting of the Theatre Royal in Nottingham. A season was only made possible in 1977 by the provision of dressing rooms in portacabins in the adjoining car park (for which the council required reimbursement for lost revenue!) The happy outcome of this was that the council acquired the Theatre Royal and instigated a major programme of improvements in 1978. Refurbishment was in the hands of the architectural practice, RHWL, and the architect leading the team, Nick Thompson, became a great champion for restoring theatres (and a frequent patron at the Coliseum). This paved the way for other regional theatres to receive similar treatment and its success in generating civic pride led to the building of a concert hall next door, thereby creating the Royal Centre. Nottingham, it should be remembered, had also opened a new playhouse the very year the National Theatre gave its first performance, quite a record to be proud of.

This was the background to the establishment of Opera North, initially English National Opera North. Local enthusiasm was strong but inevitably did not extend to an open chequebook. There was thus much negotiation with the Arts Council and Leeds City Council before the establishment of the northern company was announced in early 1978. I was involved in many of the early meetings with the local authority in Leeds and this occasioned various overnight stays at Harewood House in Yorkshire. On one occasion I recall staying in the Steward's Room below stairs and making my way up the back stairs to the Harewood 'flat' for breakfast. When a board retreat was held at Harewood I remember how we were carefully briefed on the procedure for leaving a tip for the butler. A different way of life to be sure.

With the establishment of a steering committee for ENO North (in effect a shadow board) and David Lloyd Jones as Music Director, I became less involved in the venture. The first night on November 15 1978 with *Samson and Dalila* was most memorable as far as I was concerned as Sue and I with Guy Bloomer escorted Dame Eva Turner up to Leeds for the occasion. Much of the country's musical establishment witnessed the birth of a regional opera company. Within three years the company had become independent as Opera North. In those formative years Richard Jarman, my assistant, acted as liaison officer while a member of the Coliseum house management, Roger Taylor, became Company Manager. He was succeeded by Graham Marchant. Another member of house management, Ken Baird, helped with New Opera Company admin after that company came under ENO's wing. The New Opera Company had originally been founded by Peter Hemmings while at Cambridge and had notched up a reputation for mounting new work when its existence continued with Peter at Sadler's Wells. Here, as the responsibility of Jeremy Caulton the Director of ENO opera planning, it was financially independent but could use many ENO facilities free of charge. Unlike early days at the National there was career development in the opera company!

. . . .

Enter Mrs Thatcher

After the 1974 strike it was decided that the company needed a full time personnel director and with Gerry Wood's help and much involvement by Chairman Robinson, Leon Fontaine joined the staff in the role. Leon came to ENO from WH Smith and, whilst initially we were slightly wary of him, soon became part of the team. During the 70's the political situation in the country saw price restraint, the Social Contract and other controls which all interfered with collective bargaining. Fontaine was a very skilful negotiator (and very civilised – an accomplished pianist) but even he had to contend with many near strikes. At the same time the National Theatre was faced with much disruption from stage personnel as it tried to get the South Bank theatre established (one suspected some trouble makers had progressed there from the Coliseum). The national scene and the arts world were set for a major change when Jim Callaghan's government fell in 1979 and Margaret Thatcher became Prime Minister. It was also a highly significant year for Sue and me as our son Darren was born – with no problems settling on a name this time! Further, I took on an extra-curricular post, the Presidency of the Society of West

End Theatre, which was to be of great significance for my future career in West End Theatre.

There was immediate alarm at the change in government in the arts world as it was known that there would be pressure for self sufficiency and no more state handouts. William Rees Mogg was by now Chairman of the Arts Council and sent tremors through many funded clients' board rooms. John Tooley at the ROH put it bluntly that while the government would provide all in an ideal world, reality had to be faced and it would be foolish not to seek private sponsorship to supplement inadequate government subsidy. Robinson (old Labour) had never been a great believer in sponsorship. The finances of the company at this time were extremely rocky and there had been many warnings from the Arts Council that the company was living beyond its means. It cannot be denied that we had difficulty controlling expenditure, particularly on sets. That for Aida was a nightmare. However striking Lazaridis' work was, it was expensive and caused regular nightmares for our technical director, Noel Staunton. At board level many questions were asked about financial control, making for uncomfortable times.

This was the beginning of a difficult period for the company. We had been on a roll with many productions receiving public acclaim but somehow our budgets never held and when Mackerras left for more international opportunities and was replaced by Sir Charles Groves as music director, press notices took a turn for the worse.

Mackerras had never been a great company man but had always brought out the best in those involved in pieces he was conducting – he didn't play a significant part in directorate meetings, preferring to fire off pithy memos when in residence on particular subjects. Throughout his time as director he always had international engagements and probably hankered after the role of music director at the ROH. Groves was more of a team player but, alas, not so able to get the best out of players, or so it seemed to me on the sidelines. Groves' tenure as music director was short lived and after a disastrous time in 1979 with *Turn of the Screw*, (Groves 'faltered' as Harewood put it to the board) he resigned to be replaced, in 1980, by Mark Elder. Elder, a senior member of the music staff, had been planning a period of work in Australia but was persuaded by Harewood to accept the challenge of the ENO Music Directorship role instead. Thus ended 1979 - another memorable year for the wrong reasons for the company while the country started on a new path to the right for the 80's.

. . . .

The Society and Presidency

I had resolved after the 1974 strike and management's humiliation by the SWETM conciliation board, to get to know the West End management scene and explain to them that a subsidised opera company <u>did</u> know what it was doing. This entailed regularly attending the

Society's monthly meetings as well as the meetings of the trade body for regional theatre (TMA) on a regular basis. These were held in smoke-filled rooms overlooking Leicester Square and largely consisted of reports and recommendations which had obviously been extensively discussed beforehand by the Executive, comprised of the Society's elders (figuratively and literally). The Executive then had a good lunch, all traces of which had been whisked away by the time members like myself appeared for the meeting.

I got to identify the key West End managers of the time. There was regular attendance by the ever watchful Harold Fielding and the Mousetrap Man, Peter Saunders, besides Ray Cooney, Ian Albery and John Gale. There were occasional appearances of other characters such as Donald Albery, Peter Bridge and, more regularly, Toby Rowland. The latter had been President in 1972 when I had eventually achieved membership. Rowland, originally a Broadway producer, made a considerable effort to welcome me showing the charm and warmth which served him well when dealing with producers seeking access to one of the Stoll Moss theatres over which he presided from the offices (still with coal fires in the 70s!) in the Hippodrome building along Cranbourn Street. It was always a delight to go to his office and see the slot machines which had come from one of the seaside piers Stoll Moss had acquired (and probably demolished). There was a story that these were left to Snowdon when Rowland died.

Union settlements provoked debate and those relating to the technicians union, NATTKE (later BECTU) had been carefully attended by myself before the strike. Afterwards, things improved significantly when a special committee (the Grant Aided Theatres Standing Committee) was established to monitor all settlements within the subsidised houses (RSC, NT, ROH) and check any implications for the West End. Leon, as ENO's personnel director, attended these meetings but I kept the ENO flag flying at general meetings. One hot issue in my early days was that of the Society's title. A move to drop the word 'Managers' (like adding the word 'London' a decade later) caused much discussion. I think the argument was that the word 'managers' implied it was just a body of those who wore penguin suits and stood in theatre foyers. Reformers won the day, SWETM became SWET, and ribald comments about sweat ensued – which were at least better than the previous references by critics to "sweat 'em".

There were occasional references to the generic promotion of West End Theatre (there had apparently been a report commissioned in the 60's but swiftly buried) but a real step towards the limelight for the Society came in 1975 with the establishment of its own awards. Meetings debating these were standing room only with even relatively taciturn members like myself expressing opinions. Ray Cooney regularly argued the case for the Society to have its own awards rather than relying on the long-established accolades given by the London evening paper, *The Evening*

Standard. Ray argued that an award scheme with members of the general public actually on the judging panel and with the winners' names confidential right up until their announcement at the ceremony, would give the Society a real presence. Eventually Ray's persistence won the day. The first awards ceremony in 1975 at the Café Royal, with a virtuoso performance by Albert Finney as MC, was a great success and featured in the important BBC *Nationwide* early evening programme on prime time television. In those pre-John Birt days the BBC felt it had a duty to promote the industry from which it drew so much. As the years went by and the cost of hosting and televising the Awards increased it was difficult to be sure that the resultant publicity/increased box office attendance was cost effective.

As a result of my comments around the awards, and my diligent meeting attendance I suppose, I became more of an accepted member - but it was still a surprise when I was approached about becoming President. There was much gossip about how the 'elders' of the Society 'fixed' who should hold that office but whilst members like Peter Saunders or John Gale were not averse to expressing their opinions on the subject (and many others), the process was strictly regulated by the Electoral Reform Society. Once it became known that an individual was prepared to take on the role it rarely became a major contest. I reckoned it might be an interesting challenge – it certainly proved to be that and demanding of time and patience – so I indicated my willingness to accept the office if elected and subject to

Harewood's agreement. He was more than a little surprised when I reported that I had indeed been elected and asked for his approval to accept. I seem to remember his comment being along the lines of 'Can you cope with that lot?' It was a long time before the Society's name could be mentioned without Harewood raising an eyebrow or hrmphing rather obviously.

As my time as President (its youngest to date) began in 1979 the Society embarked on another investigation into how it might play a promotional role. This was largely as a result of the success of the 'I Love New York' campaign on Broadway (witnessed first hand by many members as a result of Freddie Laker's cheap flights to the USA). Producers in the Society became very vociferous about the need for concerted action and eventually voted funding for a report on the NY Broadway activity, which included half price ticketing and generic promotions. This was undertaken (after not a little internal politicking) by a member of the Society's staff recently recruited from Equity, Vincent Burke. The resulting report (many inches thick) entitled *Ready for the Eighties* made a number of recommendations; surprisingly, the proposal which gained most support was that to set up a half price ticket booth selling at half price on the day of a performance those tickets which remained unsold at the theatre box office – with a small service fee which the Society would retain. A couple of years earlier Tony Field, the Arts Council's Finance Director, had attempted a similar operation in the recently vacated Covent

Garden Market but, having failed to do his homework with commercial managements, had drawn a blank with very few offering tickets.

The Society membership, both producing and theatre owning, decided they wanted to try to copy Broadway and voted to set up a trial in the heart of theatreland, Leicester Square. This was a major exercise. The Society had no direct experience of running anything other than an office for negotiations (the awards for a long time were run from Cooney's office at the Duke of York's theatre) and erecting even a hut in Leicester Square, though by now pedestrianised, took many hours of persuasion with Westminster City Council. Finally, the 'Booth' as it became known opened for business in 1980. Many producers waited to see what would happen before participating - but after a slow start sales took off and managers were regularly commenting favourably on the size of the queue (old habits die hard). As the booth grew in popularity its minimal facilities were always an embarrassment to me – there was barely room inside for the clerks ('boothies') let alone a visitor – thank goodness we were able to establish a relationship with the Swiss Centre in the Square for toilet facilities!

The Society's move towards industry-wide marketing brought a need for more detailed information about customer numbers and behaviour. The first audience survey (professionally conducted by National Opinion Polls) brought some ribald comments about the Society finally getting its act together with regard to marketing from *The Evening Standard* - but the information acquired allowed the Society to hold meetings with national and local government on a professional basis. Hitherto, the only facts (as opposed to hunches), that the Society had been able to quote about audiences were drawn from random surveys conducted at the Albery management box office queues on an occasional basis. Theatre producers and managers had always had considerable profile by the very nature of their business but now in a meeting with a minister hard facts could be quoted. This became very important as the campaign against VAT increases got under way.

There had been a mass demonstration organised by Equity when the new Tory government increased the VAT rate to 15% soon after taking office. The Society spent much time quoting their newly acquired facts and figures both to government and, increasingly, in response to press queries, all the while warning of the damage being done to the arts world. At first, not all members welcomed the Society speaking for the industry in this fashion, with some rather resenting the raised profile of Society staff. A significant development was when the Society fed in statistics to august bodies such as the Bank of England. All of this took much discussion and reassurance to members that sensitive commercial material was not being widely distributed and was only achieved, I recall, by the figures being processed by a respected third party - the City University - so that nothing identifiable (eg how specific shows were performing at the box office) was released. Unbelievable now when statistics in every form are the norm.

The Society had had to work hard initially to persuade Westminster City Council to give planning permission for the Booth in Leicester Square, but councillors gradually began to see the merits of working with us, particularly as a means of generating publicity. As Council leader, Shirley Porter was not slow to suggest a photo call to push a council initiative - but when that helped us too, we were happy to oblige. Porter got fed up with adverse comments about overflowing bins in theatreland at show times and decided to do something about it. This led to extra rubbish collections to clean up theatreland - all reported via photo opportunities - with funds being raised to cover the additional costs.

There were also more sensitive issues. Late night toilet facilities, or lack thereof, led to my walking around theatreland at midnight on one occasion with a senior councillor to show him the problem, which did eventually lead to temporary units appearing for periods of heavy footfall. When a need arose for a new electricity substation in the Square and it was decided to locate it underground, it was the Council which suggested that a new permanent building for ticketing (The Lodge) should surround the necessary ventilation shaft. Needless to say an appropriate memorial recorded its opening in 1992 by Porter with our then President, George Biggs.

Getting home after shows was also a problem up to the 80s. The Society was instrumental in persuading London

Transport to introduce night bus services (a promotion called 'Night Owls'). Getting late services on British Rail was more of a challenge, though our cause was helped when a mole in the organisation revealed to us the existence of late non-timetabled services available mainly for staff, enabling us at least to highlight the need for such services for theatregoers.

After various attempts to get important facts and figures about the West End across to government we sought advice from the one Society member who was also a serving MP, Tom Arnold. It was at his instigation that we appointed Fergus Montgomery as the Society's Parliamentary Consultant. He had worked for Margaret Thatcher so knew his way around Whitehall. His appointment gave us the opportunity to have certain issues raised in the Commons (however small the audience) and one or two early day motions. I don't think there were any great successes but this was new ground for the Society and the beginning of what became essential work as the role of the trade association grew.

The presidential role introduced me to public speaking which I had previously largely avoided (I went nowhere near the Union debates at Oxford). Not only were there the various launches of marketing initiatives (one saw me very early in the morning at Paddington station trying to follow a prepared script and introduce Dame Edna Everidge, who of course took over from the moment she arrived) but in my very first year the need for a speech at the Awards ceremony in a very theatrically crowded Café Royal. My predecessor as President, Ian Albery, had used the occasion the year before to deliver a forceful speech wagging a finger at the technicians who had demanded a substantial pay increase, all from a lectern on the stage. (Ian, son of Donald and grandson of Bronson, was always passionate about the West End and later made a great success of rebuilding Sadler's Wells Theatre. Years later he was involved in the planning of Nica Burns' Soho Place theatre near what was the Astoria, demolished to accommodate the new underground station at Tottenham Court Road.)

The prospect of making a similar speech terrified me so I decided to speak from my place at the table in the floor of the house and warn the government of the value of the arts now threatened by the VAT increase, carefully pointing out the support the Equity-led public march had received. Well received by the assembled thespians, of course. In my second year, Cameron Mackintosh, the awards producer, had persuaded the Society to hold the ceremony in two parts – a show featuring the award presentations at the Piccadilly Theatre followed by a celebration at the nearby Cafe Royal. This was the occasion when Olivier was given the Society's Special Award and my only speech was to ask Judi Dench to make the announcement. Much easier, though I was berated by one senior member for not fulfilling the role expected of a President - later retracted when the extensive press coverage was seen. Olivier had been elected a member of the Society in his management days and the Society was very proud of his continued membership – marked at his eightieth birthday by establishing a bursary scheme to help drama students financially each year. This activity was masterminded by producer Lee Menzies who still organises the necessary vetting process.

One of the more unusual Presidential tasks for the Awards was to attach onto each trophy a small plaque featuring the name of the winner. Since the winners were an absolute secret known only to the President (apart from our press representative who was told shortly before the ceremony), this was a somewhat tricky piece of DIY performed in a secluded spot. In 1981 Robert Morley gave me palpitations when, as award presenter and before opening the envelope with the winner's name for Best Actor in a Musical, he declared that he was convinced the winner was Michael Crawford and invited him to come and receive the award. Michael insisted that he did, in fact, open the envelope and yes, it was Michael's name, but it certainly looked as if Morley knew the outcome all along, making nonsense of the idea of it being a secret. I didn't comment to Robert on his behaviour but I certainly did to his son, my Oxford contemporary, Sheridan.

Another follow on from the 'Ready for the Eighties' report was the improvement in the London Theatre Guide. This had started life in the 1920s as a simple free leaflet listing what was on at members' theatres in the West End, but had gradually become a net contributor to the Society's income as members were obliged (pre- Office of Fair Trading days!)

to pay to list and advertise their shows. With considerable input from Peter Harlock (the extremely energetic RSC publicist, later to establish his own practice – Hard Sell) this became a more informative and comprehensive publication – but not without lengthy debate about how 'non members' should be covered. I found all these discussions about who exactly represented a particular theatre rather ridiculous but we eventually ended up with a leaflet that became indispensable to the theatregoer seeking clear what's on information – at least until the internet came along.

Probably the most important development during my Presidency was the setting up of Theatre Tokens, an idea from Pat Ide, a long standing member I had first met at Bernard Miles' Mermaid Theatre. The suggestion was that the Society should follow the example of Book Tokens with the sale of gift vouchers exchangeable in the Society's case for tickets at member theatres. After their initial but limited success solely at members' theatres the scheme was widened to other theatres. Sales too were broadened to more general outlets, including for a time Crown Post Offices (ie those directly run by the Post Office themselves). This was at a time when the Post Office was anxious to have additional items to encourage customers actually to visit their buildings. It didn't, however, produce great sales and was dropped after a short time, much to the enjoyment of Michael Codron who took great delight in drawing my attention to the Postman Pat promotions of the period. Michael was always brilliant at adding a welcome touch of humour to his interventions at a meeting whatever the subject or however critical he might be. This was the other side of the pre-eminent straight play producer of the period. He chaired with great success for many years the complex negotiations with Equity over the agreement for actors in the West End.

Initially the bookkeeping associated with the sales of Theatre Tokens was horrific – card counterfoils in shoe boxes – but with eventual computerisation the operation became a significant income stream for the Society, especially when, with interest rates soaring for money on deposit, our accountants drew up a justification for a percentage of those sales not actually being redeemed (which was always the case) to be deemed profit for the Society. This was, however, in the future beyond my time as President and when running the Society.

Looking back at my three years as President it is difficult to remember how I balanced ENO, the Society's meetings and papers (of which there were a lot!) and home life. After 3 years I decided that I should decline a further term. There was in the constitution a requirement for an election every year – the candidates being each of the members of the board irrespective of whether they wanted to stand or not. After the voting the person elected could decline the invitation to become president. Harewood had always been very willing for me to accept further periods but I reckoned I had need of more free time. There was one last activity and that was to accompany Vincent Burke - now well established as the Society's Development Officer - to New York for the Tony Awards ceremony – an absolutely exhausting weekend – when *Cats* collected an award and I visited the Theatre Development Fund's half price ticket downtown operation at the twin towers of the World Trade Centre.

Throughout my time as President of the Society, my opposite number as President of the Theatrical Management Association was Laurence Harbottle, the senior Partner at solicitors Harbottle and Lewis. On occasions it was quite daunting to have such a senior person heading up TMA but Laurence was extremely considerate and we faced a number of challenges together. My strong relationship with Laurence later led to my joining the board of Central School of Speech and Drama as well as becoming a trustee of the Peggy Ramsay Foundation, both of which had Laurence as chairman.

. . . .

Meanwhile at the Coliseum

During my presidential term if Society matters had occupied my day I had kept on top of everything at the Coliseum by working well into the evenings, which was not always popular back at home. It did, however, mean that I was very aware of ENO business and how audiences reacted to what was on stage. The early 80s saw Pountney (who became Director of Productions in 1982) and Elder setting out a new vision for the company. This was never explicitly discussed at directorate meetings (snippets came our way from casting meetings) and only incidentally at board level, but what had been an ensemble repertory company turned more towards one-off productions without long shelf life. I don't think I consciously analysed what this might mean for the company but I did start to wonder how we were going to survive the wind of financial change which clearly ruled out handouts to clear deficits. We turned more energetically to fund raising, setting up a trust (another idea from ROH) We engaged J W Thompson for an audience survey and Maggie Sedwards - a recruit from the National as head of marketing when the long serving Helen Salomon retired - spent many hours rejigging ticket prices. We heeded the Arts Council and set up a subscription scheme, engaging its great exponent, the very forceful American, Danny Newman, who was in his opinion the genius behind Beverly Sills' success at the Lyric in Chicago and who had persuaded the Arts Council of the ticket-selling benefits of such schemes with his book *"Subscribe now!"* But there was no miracle cure: the company was underfunded for the job it was doing and some began to question whether – shock, horror - London needed two opera houses. This is exactly the question which Luke Rittner as the Secretary General of the Arts Council posed in 1984 when he asked both ROH and ENO to discuss sharing a theatre.

In the meantime we relied on fundraising and appointed John Guy to spearhead the campaign. Guy had originally been appointed as the Secretary of the company's benevolent fund (an army colonel by profession, he followed two other service men in the role) and, whilst extremely efficient and good at developing the in-house corporate entertaining, he was not the one to achieve miracles. I always thought some members of the board took advantage of John's willingness to provide hospitality without requiring a clear report on any benefit from the evening. The JWT report had made it clear ENO needed more expertise and highlighted the need to recruit board members who could pull in the cash. I cannot recall any board member in my time as being instrumental in securing a major donation. One member (found by Lord Goodman) was always good for a substantial cheque from her own resources - Sue Hammerson, the widow of a successful property developer - but this was not in the same league as the donations which seemed to roll in for the ROH. I had entertained Mrs Hammerson at a ballet matinee at Goodman's request before her board role and we enjoyed good relations throughout my time with the company.

There were many high points in the early eighties. 1981 marked the company's fiftieth anniversary and it was decided to capitalise on this and fundraise with, of course, a gala and then a music marathon of fifty hours of non-stop (!) music over a September weekend. The gala on May 28 was attended by the Queen and the Duke of Edinburgh. Although Prince Philip had come to the Coliseum for a gala in 1976, this was the first time the Queen had come to an ENO performance – and we believed the first time she had met her cousin Harewood in public with his second wife, so there was much interest all round. The response to the official invitation to Buckingham Palace was eagerly awaited and it pleased me no end to be able to relay the positive acceptance received via my former secretary Amanda Nicholson who was then working for the Queen's Private Secretary. (In that role she arranged for Sue and I and our daughter to watch the Queen leave for Trooping the Colour in 1978 from the forecourt of Buckingham Palace. I am afraid the sight of HM on horseback was too much for a 3 year old Tamasin and she burst into tears.)

There had always been various lettings of the Coliseum for one-off events or galas which fell to me to handle. Of the great variety which happened in my time - ranging from a gala for a children's charity through various pop music events to the Festival Finale for the 1982 Festival of India with Mrs Gandhi - the one which stands out in my memory is that which took place at the end of the Falklands War, on July 18 1982. It is etched in my memory not so much for its content but for those involved in mounting it. When I took a phone call from Louis Benjamin of our landlord's office with an enquiry about Coliseum availability, I was very surprised given the number of large theatres in their ownership. For some reason their theatres were unavailable and Benjamin wanted to mount a show to mark the theatre world's tribute to the armed forces – in many ways reflecting similar events mounted by Oswald Stoll around WWI. It was agreed that ENO would make the Coliseum available at cost and a major exercise got under way. I was fascinated to see characters such as theatre and television director, Robert Nesbitt, and doyen of theatrical agents, Billy Marsh, in action, all skilfully directed by David Bell of London Weekend TV. I think it was the first time so many people had been backstage at the Coliseum in many a year. Benjamin obviously enjoyed himself but didn't get the public recognition in the form of an honour he perhaps expected.

Another landmark in 1982 was the Jonathan Miller production of *Rigoletto*. Miller transferred the setting to mafia-run Little Italy in New York and, when prompted, could set out how the itinerant music hall performer, Rigoletto, had fallen on hard times and become a lackey to the mafia boss the Duke. The settings by Patrick Robertson and Rosemary Vercoe were based on Edward Hopper's painting *Nighthawks* with its evocative juke box. The production became the West End hot ticket and led to Cameron Mackintosh approaching us about transferring the production to another theatre under his management. I found myself setting up various meetings for Harewood to discuss the proposal with Mackintosh and internally the pros and cons were much debated. In the end it was decided that ENO must retain this production in its rep – which it did until 2009. It would have been interesting to see how business would have fared under Mackintosh's management (It was certainly interesting to witness Harewood and Mackintosh in meetings - computers were just beginning to make their appearance in modern offices so the PC on Mackintosh's desk intrigued Harewood). A few years later Mackintosh transferred the all-male *Swan Lake* from Sadler's Wells Theatre with great success, but ENO needed *Rigoletto* business at this time – it was given a gala performance on May 15 1983 and benefited the Benevolent Fund quite substantially even without a royal presence.

. . . .

That American Tour

The first mention of a possible US tour came after a Harewood trip to the States in 1981. At this time there were often discussions with well-funded US opera companies about co-productions, so overseas trips were common to see interesting productions or singers. The resultant co-productions rarely made the budget contribution they were supposed to, but such exercises were often politically necessary.

Houston, Texas, was planning a major arts festival in 1984 and it was thought this could lead on to a visit for the company to the Met in New York. There were reports of great enthusiasm from the Governor of Texas and Harewood set off for the States with a fund-raising consultant, Princess Obolensky (an Englishwoman married to a Russian émigré living in the States – though we never told that much about her) again the following year. There were no funds raised but promises of discounts on transport and accommodation which I and many others - particularly board members - found worrying. However, the tour bandwagon began to roll. Guy, as Appeals Director, and Richard Mantle (originally recruited as Personnel Director after Fontaine's retirement, subsequently becoming Harewood's deputy) were convinced that the tour could give the company major kudos and set about making it happen. A group of very rich Americans came to London and were wined and dined at exclusive venues, while Prince and Princess Michael of Kent were persuaded by Harewood (using the family connection, no doubt) to go on a further fund-raising trip to the States - but the all-important and much quoted guarantee from Governor White of Texas was nowhere to be seen.

The merits of the tour enhancing the company's international standing, on the one hand, and its cost (estimated at one stage as $4M) on the other, continued to dominate board meeting agendas throughout 1983. Technically, the tour was to be at the invitation of the American Friends of ENO but while individual members were rich, the organisation (set up in 1981) was not. Just over half the costs were raised or guaranteed but a crucial element was some $750,000 from Governor White. At a late stage Harewood met with him and expressed to the board confidence in the Governor's ability to meet the target. Unfortunately this turned out to be misplaced and the lack of news - and funds - meant the board for some while refusing to give the go ahead. It was not until May 1984 that the tour finally had the board's go ahead. It is difficult now to be sure how the board were finally persuaded to agree but a mixture of Goodman promises (without any details being revealed) of meeting if necessary Governor

White's contribution, and the Arts Minister (Gowrie) being 'supportive', somehow overcame the doubts. I remember it as being a very difficult meeting to minute.

So it was that the tour went ahead, opening on May 24 in Houston and closing on June 29 at the Met having given performances in Austin, San Antonio and New Orleans *en route*. The repertoire was a good mix and showed the company at its best: *Rigoletto, Patience, War and Peace, Gloriana* and *The Turn of the Screw*. At first very favourable reports came back to the Coliseum of audience reaction, but there were hiccoughs with a cancelled performance in San Antonio and some thin houses. Reception at the Met was excellent so the tour ended in triumph – except for the large deficit. There were jokey comments that Harewood should chip in by selling something from Harewood House - but the serious news was that the company was going to have to work very hard to pay off the losses of the tour. Harewood attempted to get funds from Governor White but he responded that by making approaches to his contacts in the US he had done his bit! Goodman roped in a special committee and further appeals were made to government but a large financial hole remained.

Americans over here

I booked many American companies in as visiting companies. One of the most rewarding in many ways was the Dance Theatre of Harlem which I signed up for part of the opera company's absence in the States. The black company was led by the charismatic Arthur Mitchell, a former leading member of American Ballet Theatre. Mitchell exerted a strong presence on and off the stage and was widely respected by every member of the company. The season at the Coliseum coincided with the GLC's black awareness campaign and Mitchell willingly signed the company up for a special matinee for Londoners where he rather surprised some of the GLC's officials with his emphasis on discipline and formality (He was always Mr Mitchell to everyone in the company).

L-R Arthur Mitchell, director, Iltyd Harrington, GLC chair, and self at a reception given by the GLC for the Dance Theatre of Harlem during Coliseum season 1975

It was something of a plus for ENO that we had booked the company given the unhappy industrial strife of a couple of years before. It was also at the time when the GLC was waging war with Mrs Thatcher's government so any opportunity to score points in the PR battle was not lost. The formal head, Chairman, of the GLC at the time was Iltyd Harrington - a theatre devotee who made a great occasion of the whole Harlem company being entertained at County Hall.

It is worth recording here that ENO was considerably uneasy at central government's plans to disband the GLC and pass its powers to the London boroughs since the GLC provided a significant portion of its grant aid as its predecessor, the LCC, had done since the late 50s. The board member nominated by the GLC at the time, Bernard Brook Partridge, though a staunch Conservative, was vociferous in condemning the government plan. In the end the GLC's grant aid role was taken up by Westminster City Council whose member on the ENO board during my time, Roger Bramble, certainly took an active and knowledgeable interest in the work of the company – as he did in many other arts organisations, not necessarily grant aided by Westminster.

. . . .

Balancing the books

Harewood, who often digressed in meetings with amusing anecdotes, regularly referred at directorate meetings to little-known operas which he felt should be given an airing. It was in the context of dealing with very reduced budgets brought on by the US tour loss that the idea of productions with minimal settings for limited performances took hold, initially as a connoisseur series; later, when engineering company Norwest Holst were recruited as sponsors, their name was linked to the productions. (Their MD, Raymond Slater, was a significant operator in Manchester – but not, in the view of one of our board members, with an unblemished reputation!). I was one of those who reckoned that there was probably good reason for an opera to be lesser known …

Mazeppa was the first of these productions and it certainly provoked. The director, David Alden, was probably delighted but the chainsaw massacre, for instance, did not please those who had enjoyed *Rigoletto*; many left at the interval. We did please audiences at this time with productions such as Pountney's *Orpheus in the Underworld* with its Gerald Scarfe designs (expensive and late!). Other productions such as *Xerxes* (Nicholas Hytner's first opera production as I recall) and a provocative *Akhnaten* (scenery sculpted in sand … anathema to brass players in the orchestra) made it clear that the future direction was away from the more gentle style of Byam Shaw or Miller.

In the course of the many budget discussions at this time Harewood frequently commented that his successor would cost the company far more. I think it was early '84 that he announced that he would be retiring the following year and the ball started rolling to recruit a new Managing Director. Rumours abounded about who had applied following the advertisement and who the board subcommittee had interviewed. By mid-year Peter Jonas was formally appointed. Jonas was well known to Mark Elder from university days and at Glyndebourne but came to ENO from many years working in the US for Solti with the Chicago Symphony Orchestra. As MD-in-waiting, from then on he was much involved in our planning and made a number of extended visits from the US.

Harewood's farewell was with a gala in June 1985 attended by Princess Alexandra, the relation he had persuaded to become the company's patron and who took a definite interest in the company. As the person appointed to ensure her office was kept informed I knew from calls that came my way her interest was genuine – she welcomed news whether good or bad. The gala performance was followed by a company party during which Harewood was presented with the licence board from above the theatre doors in St Martin's Lane. Whilst regretting that I myself didn't acquire this public notice declaring that Harewood and Rhymes had been licensed to 'sell liquor for consumption on or off the premises', it amused me no end to think that my name would feature somewhere in the Harewood Estate in the years to come. (I kept the one before with Arlen's name and its successor identifying Jonas!)

. . . .

New boss, new directions?

Jonas made his presence felt very swiftly and set about the fundraising needed to get over the US tour deficit which he had pledged to do. Many meetings were held with the Arts Council including those with Rees Mogg who was now chairman and Luke Rittner the Secretary General (a fellow Bathonion and ex-Tory city councillor – 'one of us' in Mrs T's terms) but with limited success as far as tapping extra funding was concerned. This was, it has to be remembered, the time of *The Glory of the Garden* when the Arts Council shed a number of clients. Jonas believed the company would have to show its determination to raise funds by rattling the collecting tins (literally) after performances at the Coliseum. He set in motion the routine of there being an appeal by himself or perhaps Elder or Pountney at the end of the curtain calls. The sums raised were not significant but to Jonas the action was.

With Jonas in the driving seat I was working for someone younger than myself for the first time in my career – he was in his thirties when he succeeded Harewood. I think this and my own age with a family (!) to consider, made Sue and I take stock. We had spent some time altering my parents' house in Bath to make things easier for my Mother to maintain her independence which meant we often spent weekends there – as we did with Sue's parents in Harpenden – so weekends when there was no VIP duty at the Coliseum often saw us cramming the car full for the out-of-town experience. All of this and the prospect of our kids' London schooling led us to wonder about moving from the South Chelsea which Wandsworth had become.

Many well-heeled friends in London had found themselves second properties for weekend retreats - but we decided that life needed a complete change and I should think seriously about whether I really wanted to stay at the Coliseum. I started making my itchy feet known discreetly. We decided that we would move as a family to Bath and I would do the commuting in the belief it would of necessity reduce the number of late evenings I was working (seeing the 'house in' just in case there was someone to greet: house management habits die hard). After many viewings and almost despairing of finding anything suitable, by chance we saw an ad for a house in Bath a mile from the station offering unbelievable country attractions (one being a swimming pool!). This was Honeysuckle Farm, used by its previous owners to breed horses. Initially we had no plans to keep animals. Indeed we had little time for much thought as it was during a half term break and we were on our way further West. The house itself wasn't great but the location was, so we took the plunge and found our offer accepted. Full speed ahead with major changes.

At this time the rail service to London was fast and reliable and after our move in August 1985 I settled into being a commuter quite happily, enjoying the journey of just over an hour to read papers and plan meetings. This was fine until Jonas settled on holding major meetings at decidedly un-theatrical hours such as 08.30 a.m. It wasn't, of course, just this that made me think more about 'my career' – another mid life crisis? *Mazeppa* was clearly indicative of the new provocative style of the company and it wasn't something I was terribly happy with and able to promote. Jonas also had a way of presenting/manipulating facts that certainly made me uncomfortable - there is always the debate about whether the glass is half full or half empty but with Jonas figures - particularly those relating to attendance - tended to be manipulated to say the least. All of this coincided with some rethinking in the West End at the Society.

The organisation had been given a new emphasis with the various marketing initiatives which had taken place during my presidency; this meant that its senior employee now had a very changed workload. A solicitor by training, Bob Lacy-Thompson, the Secretary, was brilliant at detail in documents and negotiation but was not enamoured of administration or any kind of major promotion. There were therefore those in the Society who felt there should be changes when he reached retirement age. Casual conversations led to serious discussions about my possible interest in a new post of Chief Executive. The selection process would probably not be wholly acceptable today but in April 1987 I made the decision to accept the post of Chief Executive which I had then been offered and gave Jonas my resignation. He had embarked on a management study with Price Waterhouse with the aim of showing how cost effective ENO was and decided to amalgamate my admin duties with personnel and get the company secretary role undertaken on a voluntary basis (via a civil servant) - oddly enough at just the time the ROH was bringing the role in-house. It was very sad leaving the Coliseum and the great staff which I had assembled there (it's trite to talk about family but they were) but, eighteen years after joining Sadler's Wells, I felt I should seek pastures new if I wasn't to become set in my ways and probably resentful of what Jonas was trying to do.

Sue's designs for some of the visiting companies at the Coliseum

Bejart (1980)

Nureyev (1988)

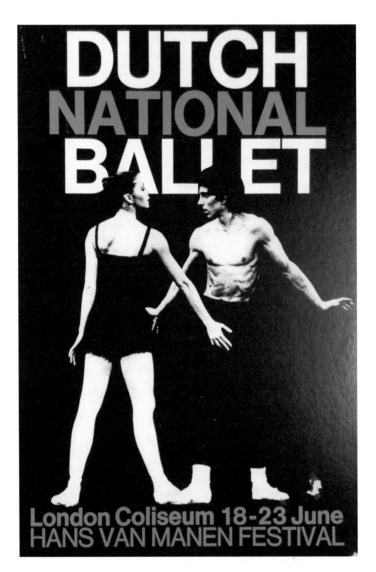

Dutch National Ballet (1984)

Royal Danish Ballet (1974)

Dance Theatre of Harlem (1984)

Sue's posters for various opera productions (SWO/ENO), the name change campaign and a promotion for Balcony sales

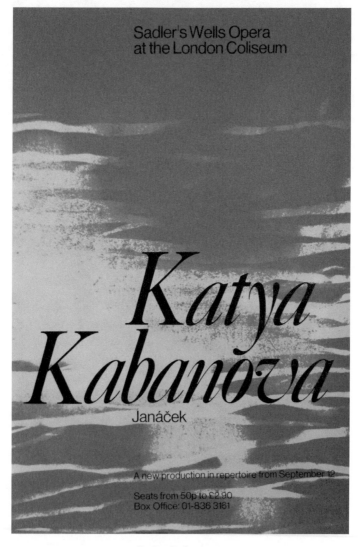

Sadler's Wells Opera
at the London Coliseum

Katya Kabanova

Janáček

A new production in repertoire from September 12

Seats from 50p to £2.90
Box Office: 01-836 3161

Katya Kabanova

Coliseum Balcony promotion

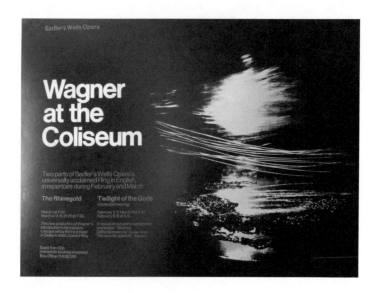

Wagner at the Coliseum

The Story of Vasco

Sadler's Wells Opera
Sadler's Wells Opera
Sadler's Wells Opera
Sadler's Wells Opera
Sadler's Wells Opera
English National Opera
English National Opera
English National Opera
English National Opera
English National Opera
English National Opera

English National Opera

Opera in English
Opera in the heart of the West End
Opera as first-class entertainment in London's largest theatre
Opera at bargain prices – seats from 50p

1974/75 Season from August 3
Booking now open

London Coliseum St Martin's Lane London WC2N 4ES
Box Office 01-836 3161

*Name change: Sadler's Wells Opera
becomes English National Opera*

Il Trovatore

The entrance to Bedford Chambers on the piazza
at Covent Garden, once home to SOLT/TMA

THE COVENT GARDEN YEARS

· ·

S o what exactly was I taking on? The new Chief Executive would run not one but two trade associations (a comparatively new description of what were often considered rather secret bodies), dealing with theatre managers and producers both in London and in the regions (which the 'provinces' had now definitely become). Henry Irving (the first actor to be knighted) had formed the Theatrical Managers Association in 1894 – or rather accepted the invitation to become president from the management fraternity. In 1908 London managers had decided that they needed a separate organisation to represent their particular interests and persuaded Sir Charles Wyndham to accept the presidency of a separate body, the Society of West End Theatre Managers. Wyndham, an actor and theatre proprietor, had in his youth combined acting with medicine, travelling to America to join the federal army as a medical officer but with breaks for acting! I am not exactly sure when the two bodies decided to share administrative staff but by the time I first came across the organisations they were firmly entwined. But they remained separate legal entities. Just to complete the picture

– or confuse further - I should point out that the TMA, by now the Theatrical <u>Management</u> Association, was the result of the amalgamation of the organisation with two others: the Council of Regional Theatre (originally, in the days of rep, the Council of Repertory Theatres) which represented those from the grant aided sector outside London; and the Association of Touring and Producing Managers who represented commercial touring producers. The resultant title TMA/CORT/ATPM was described by Guy Bloomer (of the Royal Opera House and president from 1976) as like a bad hand at Scrabble.

The amalgamations left a legacy of an incredibly complicated structure of committees designed to balance the various interests in the Association rather than achieve results. It was clearly in need of an overhaul but as I knew from my own observations as a member (for ENO) and from discussions with Guy it would be like walking on eggshells. My predecessor, Bob Lacy Thompson, as a trained solicitor liked to have a clear instruction before any action taken. Fine in an ordered office but I was used to theatres and theatre offices where things moved at speed and sometimes several things together. Bob happily prepared letters and sent them to the relevant president for signature - I caused quite a stir by actually writing, signing and dispatching such documents! I knew from my time as Society President a fair bit about how members expected their associations to be run - traditionally - many regarding the Society and TMA as akin to clubs bound by firm rules. If I was to change things

I certainly had to proceed with caution because instant change would not be tolerated and I would be out of a job.

Office technology was also of a different age; there was indeed an answering machine but as for a fax machine, which had arrived on the scene a good few years before at the Coliseum, there was an 'understanding' with a nearby office that if anything was really urgent they would help us. Members expected to be kept fully informed with written material and reams of paper were generated – I remember many battles to get proper copiers installed. During my working life I reckon technology probably advanced as quickly and profoundly as had happened in the Victorian era – calculators, PCs, laptops and mobile phones all came to be essential tools during my career.

At least the offices themselves projected a reasonable image, having been moved in 1976 to the old Covent Garden Market Authority offices in Bedford Chambers overlooking the Piazza when the fruit and vegetable market itself relocated to Nine Elms. The offices were a real change from the rooms on the sixth floor of an office block in Charing Cross Road. Covent Garden was a good central location for both London and regional members with good meeting rooms and passable spaces for staff. I say passable both because the offices and facilities (the loos were genuine Victoriana) exuded faded glory and as the area became popular the noise of buskers and street artists outside in the piazza wasn't always helpful to those working close by. The offices were originally leased from the GLC successor body and then from a private property company. Such matters as rent reviews and charges came before the Society's finance committee since the lease was held by the Society with the TMA paying its share according to a periodically reviewed - and argued – agreement.

Membership of the Society and TMA obviously entailed subscriptions. In my early days, the TMA subscription comprised a sum for personal membership and a sum to cover the theatre where the member operated. The latter was collected by a levy on the number of shows given entailing a major exercise to collect such information. The Society simplified matters by requiring an annual lump sum but, although the TMA abandoned the levy soon after my arrival, its replacement by a subscription according to size and activity of venue or management was never wholly satisfactory and there were those (who shall be nameless even in this document) who channelled their main activity through a company not in TMA membership, thereby paying a subscription related to a smaller operation. Even the major review of the organisation by Crispian Raymond in the 90s failed to address the problem. TMA membership was mainly one of organisations and only when this eventually changed to being on a personal basis did matters and the Association's finances improve.

The TMA had a small number of trading activities (in the field of training). By way of contrast, after the Society established the half price ticket booth in Leicester Square it began to see real revenue come in from the service charge on every sale, making the organisation far less reliant on subscriptions. Things improved further when Theatre Tokens went nationwide and a formula was agreed whereby a certain proportion of sales were considered permanently unredeemed and therefore could be taken as profit. (Similarly, many years previously the Book Tokens business had innocently benefitted from all the tokens lost during the Blitz).

I was very lucky with my colleagues who managed financial matters. In post when I arrived was Jim Wooldridge who had come from Stoll Moss Theatres and was steeped in that management's meticulous attention to where every penny was spent. Jim saw the arrival of computerised accounting and grappled with the new procedures required for our Leicester Square ticket booth and Theatre Tokens operations. When he retired we were able to secure the services of Martin Scott who took all that we sent his way in his stride.

But the more I think about the mechanics of office procedures in my early days the more amazed I am that we found time for anything else…

I was expected to make changes and most members accepted my moves but I had decided that evolution rather than revolution would be my approach. In the Society there were those members who were impatient for change, amongst them the very eminent producer Michael Codron, who hadn't taken much interest in the Society other than Equity negotiations during my presidency, but now spearheaded a group of producers intent on change. The group which became known as the 'Young Turks' included Nick Allott from the Cameron Mackintosh office and Andre Ptaszynski whose small independent company, Pola Jones, had logged up several successful shows. Together we hammered out a number of changes, many minor in themselves, which both helped me run the place and removed at least some of the fustiness which I had encountered at Society meetings when first a member. An amendment of the name substituting the word 'London' for 'West End' – so SWET became SOLT - helped me in speaking for the organisation with outside bodies.

TMA was a harder nut to crack. The legacy of the three sectors which had come together under Guy Bloomer's presidency – commercial touring producers, commercial regional theatre managers and subsidised managements – there really were three separate organisations originally!– was three standing committees which met regularly and often duplicated each other's agendas. Unfortunately, committee membership did not always attract the best minds and a lot of time was spent on rather domestic matters. It took several years and much diplomacy before the constitution was streamlined in 1993 and members were elected to the council of management with particular areas of responsibility. The new arrangements were generally welcomed but members of long standing made their regrets known. I was often frustrated at how long such changes took but at least they passed without bloodshed.

Trade associations were beginning to emerge as significant bodies; by the 80s the CBI had long enjoyed speaking for its members and other industries were following. Theatre producers always relied on publicity and before the arrival of the mega musicals from Mackintosh and Lloyd-Webber could only occasionally grab the headlines. Peter Saunders made the most of Mousetrap anniversaries such as celebrating a 'third of a century' at the Savoy with a glitzy lunch and could be tapped for a quote on occasions, but as the economic climate grew more difficult and the Arts Council became more in thrall to government, the subsidised managements felt it necessary to speak out in public. Philip Hedley and Peter Cheeseman regularly spoke out for the sector but rarely with any attempt to coordinate with others.

Gradually it was accepted that Bedford Chambers might speak for the industry and we began increasingly to be contacted by the media for information. I found that we were called upon for a range of facts and figures and, while this was sometimes purely anecdotal (there was the annual "Which is the most popular panto?" query), it did mean we could offer statistics about the industry as a whole thanks to the box office data we had persuaded members we could collect to provide industry information. Although West End managements had been sharing their attendance data since my presidency, it did take a lot of persuasion to convince TMA commercial managements that their precious figures could be analysed by City University in such a way that no secrets would be revealed. By 1998 the TMA Annual Report quantified the size of the UK's performing arts audience as 30 million, with 9 million tickets sold a year in TMA venues (the equivalent of 'a queue from Oxford to Beijing' - not sure who came up with that one or how it was calculated!) Often we received more attention than our size even as SOLT and TMA put together perhaps merited! This came at a price and there were tricky moments when we wished the press would go away.

One newspaper that wouldn't go away and which featured prominently in our lives was *The Stage*, founded and run by the Comerford family for over a hundred years. Unfortunately their journalists weren't highly paid and it showed in their reporting. They had a great ability to get hold of the wrong end of a stick and whatever we did to explain things we didn't always get good headlines. This may come across as sour grapes but we even had (ultimately unsuccessful) discussions with Peter Plouviez, a wonderful general secretary of Equity, about the chances of establishing a rival publication. *The Stage* then had a devoted readership of those who relied on its attention-seeking stories for inside information about the industry (theatrical landladies, perhaps) but it was the extensive - almost obligatory in some areas - advertising which was its gold mine. When the internet took over it changed their business model very significantly. Our offices were very close to those of *The Stage* which meant that we could secure early copies on a Wednesday evening and have our comments ready for Thursday publication day. There were certainly occasions when *The Stage* served the industry but it was not an easy bedfellow - though the Comerfords when directly approached were willing contributors to sponsorship appeals (the tennis match with Equity which I inherited was my first target, later to be followed up by the Regional Theatre Awards).

. . . .

Moves in new directions

The first major industry issue we faced when I was in post related to investment in theatre productions and came in the aftermath of the Barlowe Clowes insurance fiasco. Investment in commercial productions had always been conducted on the basis of a handshake/gentleman's agreement. Financial legislation passed as a result of the losses caused to investors by Barlowe Clowes' collapse meant that much more documentation would be required. I organised a number of meetings with civil servants and senior government figures explaining how our industry worked. Ministers when reached readily accepted that they had not been advised of the wider implications of the legislation before it reached the statute books. It became a long running battle but eventually a procedure was hammered out for theatre investment. Probably not entirely a bad thing that procedures replaced handshakes and casual agreements.

Another early challenge for the West End (and me) was the collapse of the long established ticket agency, Keith Prowse. With some very successful shows running in the West End, Keith Prowse had, it seemed, overreached themselves and failed to pay theatres in accordance with agreements. I first heard about the lack of payment from Peter Saunders who was a stickler for payments on the nail. KP declared bankruptcy and presented managers with the problem of whether or not to accept KP tickets for which the patron had paid KP, but for which KP had not paid theatres. They did, but after much debate. The issue was understandably a hot issue with the press and when the Society eventually agreed to honour the KP-written tickets (this was before computerisation was widespread) it led to my giving a somewhat chaotic TV interview in the melee outside the offices in the Piazza - surrounded by curious onlookers.

The year before I arrived at Bedford Chambers the Inland Revenue instructed managers to deduct income tax at source from actors' salaries. This was the subject of extended correspondence between the management bodies and various levels of the Revenue eventually reaching the Board Room at Somerset House (then the HQ of the Inland Revenue). This was a joint battle with Equity since managements recognised there would be financial implications if actors lost their schedule D status. Eventually it was agreed that there should be a test case in court.Through various contacts we were able to persuade

Andrew Park QC to accept the brief and Equity persuaded a young Sam West to be the nominated actor in the case. We were all delighted when the findings were in our favour.

But I have condensed many hours and years and should revert to the early days.

Gradually I was able to structure the office staff so as to move without every moment being checked by members or a committee. This came about by recruiting senior staff specifically for industrial relations and legal affairs. In Bob's time he had serviced every negotiation but not only did I feel this wasn't for me, it would have been impossible to take a wider view of what the theatrical trade association(s) might and should do had I been embroiled in detailed and sometimes heated negotiations. So when Harry Dagnall, one of the assistant secretaries, left in 1989 I decided to recruit someone specifically to handle the negotiations and enquiries relating to the unions on a day to day basis. Peter Morris, whom I had known as the finance officer for London Festival Ballet, headed the candidates for the new post of Industrial Officer and joined the team – and remained with me until I retired. He took to dealing with union agreements like a duck to water! There is, I am sure, something in common in watching figures and keeping on top of the details in union agreements. It would be unfair not to record that Harry Dagnall went on to a brief spell as a producer (with Bridget Hayward and a certain Edward Windsor) before finding his feet as the operations manager (known to the staff as Mr McGregor because of his knack of appearing out of the blue) for Lloyd-Webber's Really Useful Theatres, sadly succumbing to cancer at an early age.

There had been two assistant secretaries and when the opportunity arose I made the second post into that of Legal Officer. This was an obvious step to provide the legal input previously provided by Bob but it also recognised the way life was going for the theatre world. I had been amazed in my contact with American producers at how involved their attorneys had been: UK theatre was following suit and London legal practices with aspirations to serve the theatre community soon had dedicated arts teams. Programme credits to their practices soon became the norm.

My intention was to have in-house legal expertise to deal with contractual issues and comment on legislation as necessary. Unfortunately the salary I could offer meant that those recruited remained with us only for a limited time; in my later years I could show how complicated and legalistic theatre life had become (not difficult) and got agreement to improved salary levels. When I recruited a qualified solicitor, Louise Norman, from a city practice she later told me how she felt I had concentrated in her interviews about how long she would be interested in the post. Understandable, given that her three predecessors had all moved on after short tenures - one to join the Mackintosh organisation and another to marry a city high flyer.

All of the agreements negotiated by the Society and the TMA had some provision for settling disputes; that with Equity provided for matters being referred to a council made up of 3 managers and 3 Equity members with a chair alternating between management and Equity. These meetings were not that frequent but normally provided an amicable solution to a problem. When Equity was in the chair the performance was often in line with what might have been given to a paying audience. The councils ('London' and 'Provincial' for contracts negotiated by Equity) had honorary legal chairs and during my years it was a great experience to deal with Harvey McGregor and Bob Marshall-Andrews as Chair and vice chair respectively. Harvey, Warden of New College Oxford and renowned as *the* expert on Tort was a great musician and once gave a notable fund raising performance with fellow Wardens of Oxford colleges ('*Wardens in Concert*') whilst Bob delighted in his appearances in the media as the 'thorn on Tony Blair's Labour rose'. I was able to recruit Harvey to become involved with Oxford Stage Company during my time as its chair leading to some enjoyable visits to New College.

During my presidency the Society had engaged an MP to help us find our way around Westminster corridors and occasionally make comments in the House, always carefully making the consultancy position clear. After a while we had to upgrade this role – Fergus Montgomery had been replaced by the Sussex MP, Michael Marshall,- and engage as well a firm to keep an eye on upcoming legislation. This was both a sign of the times and I felt an indication that we were now playing a properly important role in theatrical life.

Politics in every sense

Politics, both with and without a capital letter, featured constantly in our work. On the national level we made a point of meeting with new arts ministers as they were appointed; previously such meetings only took place at crisis time, and until facts and figures were readily available had been rather token affairs. The background briefing before such meetings provided an opportunity to present the civil servants with information about theatre – frankly even in the arts office it was amazing how ignorant some appeared. Explaining the intricacies of theatre investment at the time of Barlowe Clowes was one thing, but general (and basic) information about how theatre management was structured, the size of the industry and the number of theatres operating was all fed in. Over time this made conversations easier, even if our offices were often doing the research for civil servants to simply regurgitate.

The TMA Scottish members in the 80s pushed for their problems to be more directly addressed and we instituted a pattern of meeting with the Secretary of State for Scotland or a senior civil servant around the members' meeting in Edinburgh at Festival time. Wales was less vociferous at this time though Jenny Richards of Cardiff New Theatre as TMA Vice President certainly made her views known.

The arts ministers during my time were an interesting group of MPs and most had a genuine interest in the arts – Richard Luce of course had plenty of time under Thatcher to grow into the job. Chris Smith came across as the most concerned about the industry at grass roots level though his book after leaving office, *Creative Britain*, isn't perhaps the greatest read.

Over the years I also came into contact with Prime Ministers: Thatcher was persuaded to give a reception at Downing Street in connection with the ENO American Tour fundraising and we were entertained, briefly, to a typical forceful address. She was herself later harangued about arts funding by Jonathan Miller when she came to the Coliseum to see his *Rigoletto*! I also attended a lecture on Millennium arts prospects with the general secretaries of the entertainment unions at Downing Street organised by Cherie Blair which did nothing to enlighten any of us but gave us an opportunity for converse with Tony. But perhaps the most impressive encounter at Downing Street was with John Major at a reception given on a day when he had already had a full day in Northern Ireland but still showed himself in full command of arts matters.

I had always had high regard for the Arts Council but as the Thatcher years passed and politics became more involved in how public money was allocated I found it more difficult to maintain the respect of previous years. Officers at the Arts Council now had less direct experience in the arts and were more anxious to spread the latest philosophy than help clients – or so it seemed. With the arrival of Roy Shaw as Secretary General from the educational world no theatre client was deemed to operate correctly unless they had an education department. As an early believer in catching them young I needed no lecture about how important theatre was to young people but what I didn't follow was the emphasis on new departments dedicated solely to this purpose. Many of the old reps had managed to run theatre in education or youth departments and found the Council's approach difficult to follow. Even today I often wonder at the emphasis placed by some organisations on their outreach activity.

Fund-raising was another area the Arts Council focussed on, whatever the size of the client. This caused a lot of problems for TMA members. The general climate of reduced subsidy in the Thatcher years was grudgingly accepted but when significant money had to be paid to an executive appointed specifically to secure donations this often upset salary scales which had been carefully crafted over years. The greatest fall out with the Arts Council came when some traditional managers were felt to be preventing their organisations from treading new paths. This was all about money: the Arts Council had a smaller pot from central government to pass on and had therefore to come up with new criteria when the available cash wouldn't go round. If a manager contested the issue then the Council began to press for his or her removal. This was never openly done but a number of managers suffered – perhaps they were set in their ways and too resistant to any change, but I never felt the Council sold itself to the arts community. Matters got worse with the arrival of the National Lottery in 1994 when the Council had to steer a course between not being able to fund clients as they needed (ie to meet their running costs) but having, it seemed, significant cash for capital work. This led to a lot of what can only be described as fudges with members spending a lot of time on form filling to access funds which were deemed to be 'new'. It also led to a number of casualties with long serving theatre directors and managers losing their jobs – and reinventing themselves as 'consultants' when National Lottery applications called for detailed reports to justify applications.

The campaign for a National Lottery was spearheaded by Denis Vaughan and he was a constant caller to my office. An Australian with a long career as a conductor, he was one of the most determined people – "Denis the Menace" to my office - I have ever met and I am convinced the eventual establishment of the Lottery under John Major was due in no small part to his persistence.

Both the Society and the TMA had delicate internal politics which had to be managed. (That's probably true of every organisation but the theatre world has some very big egos.) Both organisations had started life essentially as 'gentlemen's clubs' with business being conducted around a social gathering – or so the records I read implied. Much had changed by my time (though meetings over lunch were still very popular) but there was still a wariness of what the office might do if not fully controlled. I have already recorded my instituting a direct signature on letters and a policy of evolution rather than revolution. Changes required a lot of careful managing of personalities.

The people I reported to as Presidents of SOLT or TMA were a mix of personalities but all of them great to work with. Technically my boss was the President of the Society (and chair of the legal body, West End Theatre Managers Limited). My first President was Bob Swash, a self-deprecating champagne drinking socialist as his obituary put it, but brilliant at steering the technicalities of production for Robert Stigwood. Verity Hudson, Peter Saunders' General Manager, succeeded him but sadly succumbed to cancer early on in her presidency. She was succeeded by George Biggs who had a career at sea in the Merchant Navy before theatre management. George was a great one for one-to-one private meetings and excelled at 'having a quiet word' with officials in the technicians' union, which had become BECTU by his time. George's successor, Nick Salmon, I knew well as he had been chair of the Society's Awards Committee and responsible for producing the event during my Presidency. Besides working as an independent producer he ran for many years with great skill the Theatre Investment Fund, later renamed Stage One. This was another Goodman creation being established – as a charity somehow - to help raise funds for commercial theatre during the Jennie Lee era in the 60s. Nick was succeeded by Andre Ptaszynski who ran Pola Jones production company before joining Andrew Lloyd-Webber's Really Useful Theatres. My final boss at the Society was Martin McCallum, then a director of Cameron Macintosh's company. His attention to all that I sent him and ability to respond in the midst of all the Macintosh office activity was incredible.

At TMA my first President was Andrew Leigh who looked after with great skill the refurbished Old Vic for the Mervishes. There was then Prue Skene, the administrator at Ballet Rambert and who I had known as a secretary at the Old Vic in National days. Prue was recruited to the Arts Council after only a year as President when the Council realised it was rather male-dominated. She was followed by Roger Spence, then running the Lyceum in Edinburgh. In those pre Skype and pre Zoom days there was a lot of commuting to London! Roger was succeeded – after a contested election which was rare in my time – by Ken Bennett-Hunter, being the membership's choice over Mike Grayson who was more geared to commercial theatre and brilliantly oversaw the refurbishment of both Newcastle's Theatre Royal and the creation of The Royal Centre in Nottingham. For most of his presidency Ken worked at Theatre Royal Stratford East; balancing the affairs of TMA and the demands of Philip Hedley could not have been easy. Perhaps his regular writing for The Stage kept him sane. Ken was followed by Barbara Matthews who had managed Shared Experience for many years. My final TMA President was Maggie Saxon who had spent many years working with Peter Cheeseman, another challenging role!

All of these brought their particular interests and ideas to the role of President and I often found myself – particularly in TMA – trying to ensure the trade association workload wasn't unreasonable or causing difficulties in the paid job. After all, I could point to my own time as SOLT President to know how demanding life could be!

Very often it was possible to combine a presidential meeting with lunch or quick drink. Whilst my staff may have thought I was enjoying hospitality at notable restaurants, that hospitality was invariably mixed with trying to sow the seed of a radical change in my companion's approach to an issue, or having my ear bent about the failures of a particular strategy which the majority favoured. Over the years I probably lunched with Peter Saunders the most. I knew how he cared about the industry and the changes he had seen as an aspiring producer – I had read *The Mousetrap Man* very thoroughly! I say lunch, but for Peter that was a couple of glasses of champagne and a smoked salmon sandwich interspersed with much reflection about the industry. Peter may have been considered a dinosaur by some and resented for his apparently wide influence, but his accounts of battles with Binkie Beaumont and other establishment figures when he was starting out as a producer made you realise he had certainly once been a rebel himself and suffered many setbacks in a varied career before his success with the *The Mousetrap.* You realised from his conversations just how much his skill contributed to the longevity of *The Mousetrap* whatever its literary merits. He was certainly a different person when at home with his wife, Katie Boyle. Another wonderful character with a career as varied as Peter's – and even more headlines!

Whilst the organisations steered clear of members' disputes with one another, someone had to try and avoid such issues escalating – and that was invariably me. There were members who very skilfully operated as one entity in membership but another when their business procedures did not conform to best practice or follow agreed union agreements. No names, no pack drill as the saying goes. Theatre production and management often needed those involved to take enormous risks and perhaps sail close to the wind; all having an impact on the trade association. Of course, showdowns could have been allowed to happen but would they really have helped resolve the issues? I thought not.

. . . .

And the winner is...

The high point in the Society's 'social' calendar for much of the time was the annual Awards, originally under the Society of West End Theatre Managers banner but after careful negotiations with the family in which I played a small part, the Olivier Awards. What started out as a fairly intimate occasion at the old Café Royal in Regent Street moved on to become an American Tony style event at a theatre with a reception in the Great Room at Grosvenor House. The Awards always generated interest/controversy, sometimes promoting the industry and selling more tickets. However much the awards categories were debated, each ceremony brought claims that a significant aspect was being neglected. I had been on the receiving end of one of these complaints as Society President from Andrew Lloyd Webber and reckoned the categories would always have to maintain fluidity!

When the awards were set up under Ray Cooney they were unusual in having members of the public on the judging panels along with 'professionals' eg representatives of Equity, of the drama schools and from broadcasting (Roy Plomley, the originator of Desert Island Discs, served for many years as a panellist and was fun to deal with). Selecting these people fell to an awards committee which oversaw the whole event – finding a producer, presenters and selecting the menu for the post awards meal (much debated!) After Ray gave up involvement the committee was for a time jointly chaired by Eddie Kulukundis and Cameron Mackintosh, the latter concentrating on the details of the entertainment which surrounded the awards' presentations. For Cameron, a temporary stage in the large room at the Café Royal was not the place to present even a taster of what the West End had to offer, so he was not content until a real theatre was used. This in turn brought its own problems.

There was invariably uncertainty about the availability of an appropriate theatre and the biggest question of all, would the BBC cover it? The first presentation had featured in part in the magazine programme of the time (Nationwide), but as years passed the Awards grew and received full programme status helped by the support of Bill Cotton. But costs also grew so that when Bill Cotton retired from the BBC the Awards were no longer a definite fixture in their schedules and had to be argued for each year. This involved high level (ie sixth floor at old BBC Centre!) negotiations and was helped when the Society's president had business there: Andre P with his light entertainment connections (he was a major player in Red Nose Day activity) always got attention if not guaranteed transmission at peak viewing time.

The essential ingredient in the Awards budget was support from a sponsor and here there was constant uncertainty. Sponsors wanted their product's name in lights with as many editorial mentions as possible not to mention visual and incidental exposure; the BBC, however, had a raft of rules about how a sponsor could be mentioned (codified, I think, by Cotton himself) and invariably the sponsor adjusted their contribution according to the exposure they had been given in the previous ceremony. For a number of years The Observer under Donald Trelford's editorship chipped in but it was always a tight budget. In my last years, at the instigation of Robert Fox, the Society entered into an agreement with consultants Quintus to develop sponsorship opportunities but this never flourished largely because the majority of members were out of tune with what sponsorship in the modern world entailed. We moved through a range of sponsors: Benson & Hedges (yes!), Gordon's Gin and

American Express. It was a feeling within the board that moves to appoint a range of companies as 'the official suppliers of x,y,z to the Society' via the Quintus agency would upset headline awards sponsor Amex that stymied any real progress in that direction. In later years (after my time) a rival credit card company moved into sharing the Awards title, no doubt writing a significant cheque to get the 'in association with' as part of the billing.

It is worth recording what form the physical award presented took. Initially, because it hadn't been a high priority in the planning, the award was an 'off the peg' Wedgwood urn which needless to say led to some unflattering comments about pots from winners. After various suggestions that something should be commissioned from a contemporary artist (Bob Swash tried to get support for commissioning Barbara Frink during his presidency), Alan Davis (director of the long running farce *'No Sex Please, We're British'*) did eventually secure support for commissioning a bust of Olivier as Henry V in the Old Vic production of 1937. This has now established itself as The Award.

Running the awards operation – from arranging tickets for the judging panellists through to organising the social side of the event itself - involved considerable administration, and I was fortunate in having on the staff someone who could cope with all the egos involved, Olivia Pugh. Whilst the awards were a Society activity, I was able to structure Olivia's work so that she also covered many tasks for TMA. I always felt that as long as the interests and costs of each organisation were correctly accounted for it was better to blur a few distinctions as to who worked for who. I also believed that the chief executive's role was to facilitate behind the scenes rather than to grab the spotlight: I didn't initially give myself a credit in the Awards brochure despite spending many hours resolving tricky issues. A number of producers tried their hand at producing the awards, some more successfully than others, though none matched the early achievements of Mackintosh in the Café Royal. To be fair, that was a far more intimate event on which television seemed to be eavesdropping rather than the show for television which it later aimed to be with a nominated BBC producer.

The profile achieved by the Society through the Olivier Awards led to many in TMA hankering after their own awards. From my earliest days a great campaigner for these was Andrew Leigh who hankered after the TMA creating the 'Irvings' to rival the 'Oliviers'. Although this didn't come to pass, we did, in fact, initiate a ceremony in 1991 when I was able to persuade my old contact at Martini to provide some support for a couple of years. TMA members welcomed the opportunity to meet *en masse* since, unlike their West End contemporaries, they were not in regular social contact with one another. The TMA quarterly meetings were important in this respect especially as they became associated with a glass of wine. There was also an annual conference but this tended to be dominated by members from the subsidised sector until we found a way of adding some additional interest. This was where the awards fitted in.

The first presentation in 1991 was in Sheffield and must have smoothly as I have no particular memories of the occasion! Although Martini sponsored a further year of awards they made it clear that they were not continuing and we had to look around.

With the help of Bill Cotton, now retired from the BBC but with much involvement in the regional independent television companies that then still existed, we were able to get Anglia Television to put an awards programme together but this only worked when the conference was in Norwich and we then had to find other excuses for a Norwich event. By this time the sponsorship scene had changed and we were involved with Barclays Bank who were supporting regional activities with Arts Council involvement - with much supervision by sponsorship consultants Kallaways on behalf of Barclays. Judging was not a simple operation and the voting somewhat casual, relying as it did on locals to take the initiative and vote about their theatregoing (certainly not getting the guaranteed free tickets on offer in the West End for the Olivier Awards judging panels) In all honesty I found the voting procedure something of a fudge but our members certainly made the most of the results.

Out to lunch

As the Olivier Awards became more of a large-scale occasion there was a move to reinstate something of the more intimate social event of Café Royal days for Society members. Michael Codron and David Conville suggested a periodic lunch in a London restaurant with a notable chef (Marco Pierre White was a hot favourite in early days) and this was enthusiastically adopted. The 'foodies' as they became known, tracked down some great locations and wonderful food (at skilfully negotiated prices of course). Codron always managed to end matters with a ditty wittily reflecting current business or personalities. He sometimes passed hilarious notes across the table at meetings guaranteed to throw the recipient off course if in the middle of some serious reporting, perhaps light relief to his regular role as a top producer.

TMA scheduled a formal lunch around its annual general meeting.These lunches were a challenge to arrange especially after the demise of the roof garden at Derry and Toms; my attempt to be radically different at the Imagination Gallery some years later was, I'm afraid, a disaster since members were not ready for limited quantities of *haute cuisine* on designer plates. We did, however, score with the members' quarterly meeting in November being scheduled to coincide with the arrival of Beaujolais Nouveau!

*Sir Henry Irving's statue in Charing Cross Road receiving
a tribute on January 24 1994 from Sir Derek Jacobi
and a member of London Festival Ballet to mark TMA's
Centenary – a very wet occasion, hence my umbrella*

As an historian I always had an eye for important dates (still do) and in 1988 the Society celebrated its 80th year with a members' lunch at the Hyde Park Hotel where it had originally met – though even with Codron's negotiating skill we didn't achieve 1908 prices. In 1994 TMA celebrated its centenary. On Irving's birthday the newly knighted Derek Jacobi laid a wreath on Irving's statue opposite the Garrick Theatre and a large group of members and TMA staff with the then Minister for the Arts, Peter Brooke, marked the centenary at a lunch at the Savoy Hotel.

In early 1999 I received a rather surprising invitation to go to Buckingham Palace to discuss how the Queen might spend a day seeing the West End at work. The call was from the Queen's Assistant Secretary, Mary Francis, who I learnt had instigated a programme of events so that the monarch might see important industries at work rather than just making an official and probably boring official visit. I duly went along to the Palace and found myself involved in the detailed planning of the Queen's diary for the day. Various visits to rehearsals and workshops were discussed and then there was the matter of lunch. There seemed to be only one real contender – the private room at The Ivy (then at the height of its fame) – and I bravely suggested that the Society would host and arrange this. I had no difficulty in getting Andre Ptaszynski and the board to agree to my proposal but what proved more challenging was the invitation list. Board members, yes, but what about other significant industry players from the commercial side of the industry?

The added complication was that the invitations were to be for individuals not couples. Most accepted, but one member decided he wouldn't come alone – until the morning when he suddenly decided he would. The event went well (apart from a waiter spilling sauce down the back of Paul Elliott's jacket!) and the Queen and Prince Philip (who used his green London taxi for his travel that day) seemed to enjoy the company at lunch. There was a presentation of champagne glasses with the Society's logo but I noticed Andre's assurance that they were dishwasher friendly failed to raise a smile from Her Majesty... In the evening the Queen and Prince Philip caught up with *The Lion King* which brought more news coverage than the rest of the day.

. . . .

The battle of the airwaves

In 1993 Andrew Lloyd-Weber produced *Sunset Boulevard* at the Adelphi Theatre with a complex set which relied on wireless controls rather than manual labour to move around. Although the Society rarely got involved in production matters, this show's use of radio air waves raised issues which brought about my involvement with radio microphones. The controls for the set used certain radio frequencies which, unfortunately, were also being used by others, including the London taxi network. This led to a series of highly technical discussions with government bodies before the separate needs of all using the limited radio spectrum were recognised. One meeting at the RCA (the government's relevant agency) brought together a wide selection of West End management technical personnel including a junior member of Lloyd-Weber's office, Edward Windsor, then in his theatre 'apprenticeship'.

John Byrne's cartoon for The Stage highlighting the problem with availability of airwaves for the use of radio mikes

It was eventually accepted that the needs of live entertainment in all its forms had to be recognised and the management of the relevant spectrum was passed to an independent agency, JFMG, who collected the license fees on behalf of government, operating as a commercial company (in many ways along the lines of the DVLA).

Since I was the spokesperson for the theatre world I was asked to join the licensing company and spent some time at meetings constantly ensuring theatre interests were protected. My time with the organisation coincided with the merging of the various commercial TV companies under the Granada and Carlton banners as ITV plc, providing me with a fascinating opportunity to observe these major players in the broadcasting world. Eventually ITV decided they would handle matters in-house and ended the involvement of independent directors like myself. Ensuring the interests of the entertainment industry were recognised by those allocating radio frequencies soon became a major issue and features now on international agendas.

. . . .

Across the pond

I had paid my first visit to New York in 1982. When Andre Ptaszynski became Society President in 1997, he felt strongly that we should learn more about how Broadway had demonstrated its value (in addition to its cultural worth) to the City of New York and beyond. Crucial for this was their compilation of an economic impact report showing quantitively the scale of Broadway theatre's contribution to the economy of the city, state, and country. Unlike 1982 I was able to secure the board's enthusiastic agreement to my spending a week there! Besides learning how the study had come about, it enabled me to investigate the *Broadway Live* campaign, then in full swing, which had been masterminded by Jed Bernstein (a true exponent of American self-promotion) the CEO of the Society's counterpart, the League of American Theatres and Producers. I saw a large number of shows, mainly musicals. I am afraid I never really fell for NY in the way many of my compatriots did. I am probably too 'English' and cannot take the brash approach adopted by some Americans! The week also enabled me to discuss the then hot topic of British actors appearing on Broadway with some of the leading managements – the British mega musical was making its mark and American Equity were unhappy. Those discussions did no more than set the scene for further lengthy discussions which continued beyond my retirement and entailed my successor making many trips.

It was a crowded and exhausting week and I came back determined to pursue producing an economic study, and also to spread the idea of business improvement districts, BIDs, – a form of self-help for areas where local authority action just wasn't enough to create a pleasant hospitality environment. (The Times Square BID was at that time transforming that previously rather seedy area). Whilst BIDs took some while to develop in the UK, beginning to appear now (2023) in the West End of London and even in Bath, the economic impact study found favour immediately. The Society already had much statistical material and we were able to secure the input of Tony Travers (a senior LSE figure who was regularly quoted by the press on London's economic life) to bring the material together. A key player in the exercise was Paul James who had joined the Society's staff in 1996 as Commercial Manager. This appointment was enthusiastically endorsed by Martin McCallum from the Mackintosh office who had succeeded Andre as President. It is appropriate to record that the Society had made a number of efforts to promote the industry in the 80s and 90s with active participation in tourist trade and public events spearheaded by Susan Whiddington as Development Officer - but these were not getting through to higher attention and it was this which we felt we had to address.

The two year process was completed in 1998 and the findings published under the heading of *The Wyndham Report*. Chris Smith at the DCMS welcomed "the message it conveys about the economic importance of West End theatre as well as its valuable contribution to the wider debate on the future of the creative industries" while one of his predecessors, Virginia Bottomley, was "delighted to see the contribution [West End theatre] makes to our economic life so well documented".

Besides making clear the importance of the industry, what were we asking for? A long running issue (from Barlow Clowes days) was that of simplifying commercial theatre investment. We also sought more support for those regional and non-West End theatres providing a breeding ground for new work, and recognition that the bricks and mortar of the capital's theatre infrastructure represented a national asset that should be treated as such. A tricky message to get across when several producers were trumpeting unprecedented success. These aims were strenuously pursued in my final years at the Society and certainly the matter of the state of theatre buildings in the West End followed me in retirement to the Theatres Trust.

. . . .

Touts and TKTS

When the Leicester Square Half Price Ticket Booth opened in 1981 we recognised that its title was a mouthful but felt it was important to explain exactly what it did. For a long time this worked well but gradually a number of agencies decided they would also sell reduced price tickets as a result of securing these as part of deals with managements. This led to there being a proliferation of outlets for 'half price tickets' in and around Leicester Square all claiming to be 'official' in some way. In New York the discount operation in Times Square operated under the banner of TKTS and I spent some while after my return trying to come to an agreement with the League to use those same letters because it could be registered as a trading name unlike 'official' which anyone could claim to be. In addition, as the likes of *Cats* and *Phantom of the Opera* became hot tickets, the issue of ticket touts was rarely off the agenda – discussions taking in disparate figures such as Harvey Goldsmith and the luminaries of Wimbledon tennis. In fact, it was shows falling off the hot list rather than any formal success by the Society which reduced touts to the level of irritant rather than major problem. After all, if someone really wanted tickets why shouldn't they pay whatever was demanded for them on a particular night?

. . . .

Conferences and TMA's aspirations

An annual conference wasn't a regular feature in the TMA calendar until the Regional Awards came on the scene. Certainly participation in any weekend activity was pretty rare as far as my predecessor was concerned - but to me it represented a chance to learn more about how regional members operated. David Jackson, the TMA representative for Scottish Opera and Glasgow's Theatre Royal (and one-time box office manager at the ROH and National) promoted the idea of an extended conference in Glasgow in 1990 (the year when the "Glasgow's Miles Better" promotion flourished…) and with the city's PR chief, Eddie Friel, came up with a very successful programme. The opening address was by Peter Brook and dwelt on the reserved occupation of a piano tuner in WWII and by extension the importance of the arts in society – well, that's how I remember it! The closing speech was similarly provocative from Peter

Plouviez, the General Secretary of Equity. (His cartoons of participants in any meeting were real treasures!). The Glasgow Conference was also significant for me as it provided introductions to speakers from the Netherlands who went on to provide the impetus for the creation of the performing arts employers' association in Europe (Pearle).

Signing the TMA-Equity agreement with Peter Plouviez, General Secretary of Equity, 1988 (image courtesy of Conrad Blakemore).

Glasgow also marked the emergence of strong voices within TMA seeking greater influence and rather more out of their association than just industrial relations (though they had already had that and more in my opinion). The problem was that there wasn't enough money to do all they wanted. Certain members had already (even before my time) run a marketing course based at a fun hotel,

Druidston, in Wales, but more was wanted. This all came to a head when Ken Bennett-Hunter became President and set about finding funds for a new, dedicated TMA member of staff. Early attempts in this direction (I think in Laurence Harbottle's presidency in the 70's) had not been successful but I agreed that we should give it a go. I probably made a mistake in agreeing to the designation "Senior Executive Officer" but we were lucky in finding a former stage manager, David Emmerson, who worked for Peter Wilson, producer of long-running thriller *The Woman in Black* and director of the Theatre Royal in Norwich. David eventually settled into the office set-up very well but an awful lot of his work was keeping members happy and coping with the mundane. There remained those members such as Peter Cheeseman and Philip Hedley who were only really happy if they themselves responded direct to journalists with sound bites which could get media attention.

The Office Search

A consequence of the success of Theatre Tokens was that with careful accounting (taking into 'profit' those unredeemed tokens) the Society became financially affluent. Compared to the early days when the Society had to decide which creditor to pay first this was unheard of! It led to Stephen Waley Cohen, who chaired the Society's finance committee, suggesting that I might start a search for freehold premises in the West End. As I put it to a subsequent meeting, this was akin to trying to find a bungalow amongst high rise developments – there were very few premises giving the kind of accommodation we needed.

The staff at the entrance to the Rose Street offices at the start of the new Millenium

The search took the best part of a year before, in one of my late night wanderings around the nearby alleyways - Sue and I had taken the plunge and leased a flat in Covent Garden - I found a rather dilapidated building alongside a hostelry, The Lamb and Flag. The pub had flourished in the days of the Covent Garden Market and had subsequently found a new life due to its great location off busy Garrick Street. The important fact about my 'find' emerged later – that the property was in the portfolio of a company which had up the family tree a director who had worked for Lord Goodman. We discovered that the property was not that significant to its owners and after inevitable hitches we were able to make an offer for the premises through our agent – Richard Deeble Rogers of local agents EA Shaw - who really knew his Covent Garden. However, the property survey showed that the roof of the second floor was in very poor condition which led us to consider adding a floor. That in turn suggested subletting part of the premises with inevitable protests from the Covent Garden Community Association about adding the floor. After much hassle and not a little building upheaval the Society owned bricks and mortar in Covent Garden. Quite a feat. For the second time in my career I had secured a significant property purchase for my employer.

As we set about the move we had to negotiate 'dilapidations' with our Bedford Chambers landlords and I rather wickedly suggested to our agent that if he secured agreement to a particular figure we would give him lunch

– in Paris! With that incentive he of course succeeded and as I used it as an occasion for a Pearle meeting, everyone was happy.

· ·

More campaigning

By the time John Major's premiership was drawing to a close there was a lot of discontent in the arts world. This had led some to set up an 'arts awareness campaign' and when Stuart Steven, editor of the Evening Standard, became the campaign's chairman its profile and effectiveness rose. I had actually suggested Stuart for the post having witnessed his speech at an Evening Standard Awards presentation. The campaign's director, Jennifer Edwards, left shortly after the '97 election (possibly expecting a political appointment, I thought) and a new broom was recruited by Stuart, namely Victoria Todd. She brought a new dimension to the campaign and made the whole unit more professional. It was funded from donations from the unions and the management bodies and a number of partnerships with others. Victoria was from the arts world (having run CDET and been a member of the Tate staff) and made contacts and friends across the political spectrum to great effect.

. . . .

Across the Channel and Beyond!

Andrew Leigh, President of TMA at the time of the Association's Glasgow Conference in November 1991, had been very keen on giving it an international dimension and as already mentioned we secured two good speakers from the Netherlands, Rudolf Wolfensberger and Jaap Jong. Their theme was the importance of cooperation within the EU and Rudolf stressed the desirability of a united front on a campaign for a reduced rate of VAT for cultural activity. It was this subject that saw him visiting my office *en route* to the ABO (Association of British Orchestras) conference shortly afterwards – Rudolf ran the equivalent Dutch organisation whilst Jaap ran that for theatre companies. I was probably rather dismissive of the whole VAT campaign (I had made a feature of the strength of feeling on the VAT increase back in 1979 as President of the Society and become despondent of it getting anywhere). Rudolf made a strong case for arguing a general arts case to the European Commission and I gave my support, little expecting anything to result.

Early in 1991 I heard more from Rudolf: an invitation to a conference in Amsterdam to discuss such cooperation further. Typical of Rudolf was the associated request, could I provide someone to minute the meeting? I volunteered the services of our Legal Officer, and found the meeting more productive than expected. Rudolf had assembled representatives of various arts employers' organisations from Sweden, Germany and France. We resolved to form an official body, spending rather a lot of time working out the organisation's title (Pearle, the Performing Arts Employer's League Europe) and leaving our host with a fair amount of homework. We should have realised that the Dutch were good at making contacts even if not so keen on the follow up. We met again that autumn and started formalising things; by the time we met in Stockholm in 1993 we had a formal constitution, in French and English. We also had acquired representatives from Belgium, Parisian commercial theatres (somewhat similar to SOLT and with an Englishman, Stewart Vaughan, on the staff who had worked for Ray Cooney at one stage in his career), Italy, Norway, Denmark, Austria, Switzerland and, later, Hungary. More important than the number of organisations involved was the seniority of those participating. Rolf Bolwin, the Director of Deutsche Buhenverein (German theatres and orchestras) later admitted that he had initially been sceptical of Pearle but gradually realised the significant role it could undertake and throughout most of my time attended with his legal officer.

Over the years Pearle managed to achieve recognition by many departments of the EU and more general European bodies such as the International Labour Organisation. It is now accepted as a significant player alongside the international arms of the performers, stage unions and musicians and led to the formation of bodies such as Opera Europe. It became an important player amongst international arts management bodies and I feel privileged to have been a founder member and president for a number of years, meeting some wonderful people and visiting many great cities, often at significant times such as the early days of post-Cold War life in Budapest and Tallin.

Another diary appointment I gave little attention to at the time was that made by Jan Stoneham who wanted to talk about the origin of the Olivier Awards as she was setting up a similar scheme in Australia under the banner of Robert Helpmann (who had produced that *Peter Pan* way back at the Coliseum). In fact, the meeting lasted a very full morning and covered every aspect of the work of SOLT and TMA. Jan expressed interest in Pearle and I undertook to make an introduction to Rudolf quite expecting that to be way in the future. Not at all. Jan wanted the introduction asap and before long she had invited herself to the next conference, in Helsinki as I recall. She gave a forceful presentation (very Australian) and took particular interest in copyright law negotiations, then in the process of extending copyright protection to 70 years after the death of the author/composer.

Jan also spoke about her intention to hold an international conference in Melbourne and hoped I would attend. I thought that this was one of those invitations which would never materialise but I had misjudged Jan. As the months passed into years the conference regularly featured in conversations we had over meals when Jan visited London. I often wondered about these long visits to

Europe but whatever personal reasons there may have been, it was clear both from Jan and other antipodean visitors that if they were visiting Europe it was a long way and worth making a full trip. Lord knows how many air miles she logged up.

After I returned from my summer holiday in 1998 I was amazed to find the conference invitation had actually arrived. I had never really thought seriously about going to Australia – though both Sue and I had a number of friends there and the Sydney Opera House always beckoned. Sue and I wanted to take a full break but needless to say the office diary ruled out any break longer than two weeks. We did take in Sydney (and the Opera House) as well as a delightful stay in Cairns before hitting Melbourne. The Conference was concentrated into a very full day and overflowed with international speakers. Jed Bernstein from the League gave a polished repeat of his Live Broadway presentation and I particularly recall the account of the construction of the theatre in Singapore (where we broke our flight on the way home and dined at Raffles Hotel) - but I think the conference was more of an achievement in gathering people together than a significant arts discussion.

Another unexpected trip was that I made to Moscow for the World premiere of the musical *'Tomorrow Land'* in September 1999. This followed an invitation from Charles Stephen, the brother of a former Coliseum colleague, who had obviously found or convinced some Russians benefitting from changed economic climate, of the joys of theatrical investment. An enjoyable weekend but I wasn't surprised that the production didn't transfer anywhere.

• •

Alma Mater

During my time with SOLT/TMA I had little time for much 'outside' activity but I was involved with Mander and Mitchenson as already mentioned and, for a decade, with a TMA member company as its chairman. This came about as a result of a call from Dick Linklater who had been the Drama Director at the Arts Council (in its 'better' days) and had been persuaded, largely because he lived nearby, to take on the chairmanship of the Oxford Stage Company, then resident at the Playhouse. I had had much contact with Dick during my time at the Old Vic and he thought as an Oxford man I might enjoy being associated with the place again.

Well, there were certainly enjoyable moments and many challenges. At an early stage we had to recruit a new artistic director and were lucky in securing John Retallack who conceived a number of triumphs for the company. It was with the OSC that I gained real experience in handling people giving their free time to the arts but using all their expertise and contacts. With the OSC I was also on the receiving end of the Arts Council's requirements, thereby having to comply with policies which in my paid employment I was often opposing. It was nonetheless a great experience and when we were assessed by the Arts Council towards the end of my regime they were very complimentary about my work. ("The Board is led with great clarity and expertise by Rupert Rhymes.")

. . . .

Retirement beckons

I am not exactly sure when I first fixed in my mind the idea of retirement, but by the time Martin McCallum had taken on the Presidency of SOLT (to be technically my boss) I felt I had begun to have had enough. I had served six Society and five TMA Presidents by the time the dreaded Millennium approached. Each was different and enjoyable to work with, some being high profile managers, others quiet negotiators. Martin was keen on bringing the two bodies closer together to address many of the issues facing theatre in the widest sense. There was also a desire to include the smaller scale 'independent' managements who had their own organisation, ITC (Independent Theatre Council), with which I had regular contact over the years. To an extent the *Wyndham Report* was key in keeping issues live: new writing, theatre buildings, investment in commercial productions - all featured in discussions, formal and informal amongst the bodies. But there was also a feeling that more 'joined up' thinking was needed, the comparatively recent arrival of the world wide web and creation of a London Mayor also playing their part.

An important impetus to take stock of relations and opportunities, of course, had been the election of a New Labour government under Tony Blair in 1997 but there was a certain amount of suspicion about what 'New' would bring or when this might get picked up by the Arts Council (which was fast losing the respect of the arts world). After much discussion the plan was formed for there to be a major theatre conference from March 1 to 3 2001 to set out the issues which dominated theatre life: who exactly was theatre for, where was the audience of the future coming from, and what could be done about theatre buildings themselves? The conference - 'Theatre 2001 – Future Directions' - kicked off with a thought provoking address by recently retired NT Director, Richard Eyre, neatly addressing those questions. His comment about the less-than-ideal customer experience in many theatres stuck in my memory: "It's like sitting in an Anderson Shelter in the Imperial War Museum as part of the Blitz Experience."

At times some of us wondered if we would ever get through the conference; that we did was largely through the skilful direction of Rosy Runciman as Programme Director. The conference was a success and logged up considerable publicity for the industry but we all felt the important thing was to ensure issues were followed up. To pursue this we published the full proceedings (edited into a cohesive whole by Rosy) with a very clear set of recommendations from Dominic Shellard as the Conference Rapporteur. These ranged from improving training, following the lead of the cinema industry by not being afraid to publish audience figures, and, music to my ears, addressing the heritage problem by bringing the physical environment of 19th century theatre buildings up to the standards of the current century. Two issues dominated my life in the following months - the state of the West End building fabric and where new product would come from – that is until 9/11.

That was another date destined to remain in the memory. There was a publicity event at the Booth at lunchtime (launching the acceptance of credit cards) and I had agreed to attend a reception that evening in the City. Arranged by London First (one of the organisations set up to promote business in the capital) it turned into a very morbid occasion. I remember standing around with others not quite believing what we were hearing of the news. Suddenly everything had changed and no one could come to grips with what the future might hold - I had vivid memories of the ticket office I had visited back in 1982 in the base of one of the Twin Towers.

Very slowly life became somehow normal – the TMA President Barbara Matthews visited New York but it was some while before any Americans visited us. A sad consequence of 9/11 for me was the abandonment of the League's conference that year which had been scheduled to be held in Cuba. (I had attended a previous conference of theirs in New Orleans thereby following in the footsteps of the ENO tour of 1984 which I had not joined because of Coliseum duties.)

*Conference of the League of American Theatre
and Producers, New Orleans 1999. L-R Paul James,
Jan Stoneham, self and Jed Bernstein*

So 2001 drew to a close in a rather different way to that which I had been expecting. As the months passed I found myself being wined and dined quite a lot. There was also a letter from No 10 asking if I would accept an OBE. This I duly received from the Prince of Wales; I remember following Dennis Quilley in the queue to be honoured and the Prince commenting "Ah - another theatrical recipient". It was fascinating to go 'back stage' at Buckingham Palace but one did notice the areas which could have benefitted from some re-gilding!

At Buckingham Palace to receive my OBE July 12 2002

The SOLT board gave Sue and I a great dinner at the Garrick with a typically witty contribution from Michael Codron, while in the early days of retirement there was a reception on the Old Vic stage given by both SOLT and TMA. I even got a special Olivier award from the Society at the 2002 ceremony.

*Sue and I surrounded by Pearle colleagues at my
retirement party on stage at the Old Vic January 2002*

When and if I stopped to think about the future, I did
wonder how I was going to spend my time... but I already
had a few ideas and approaches. Above all, surely it would
be good to enjoy West Country life.

As retirement came nearer I reflected on how the
arts world had changed during my professional life. The
most striking change was in the standing of the Arts
Council, no longer with the universal respect of former
days nor employing those who naturally earned respect
with experience of actual employment in the arts world.
My own organisation - now firmly recognised as a trade
association rather than a male-dominated club – had evolved
significantly and would go on doing so. I had made some
improvements – achieved by 'evolution not revolution' –

and could look back on new organisations like Pearle as well as others changed out of all recognition. I took no part in the appointment of my successor and smiled when the headhunting firm appointed to identify possible candidates told me I would be a hard act to follow. I also knew that whoever was appointed wouldn't have wanted the job I took on in 1986! SOLT and TMA were no longer cosy clubs run by a few influential characters but were well on their way to being significant forces in the theatre world.

GROWING OLD IN BATH - ALL WORK (AND LITTLE PAY!)

Enjoying life on the farm

My first project in retirement was a personal and domestic one. We had made a number of alterations to Honeysuckle Farm over the years but now decided to take a comprehensive look at what existed in the two-up, two-down farm workers' cottage we had bought in 1986. The biggest change had been in 1992 when Sue took the bold step - and major career change - of starting a boarding cattery. This idea originated during a wine filled meal on holiday with friends the year before when the conclusion for balancing household accounts had been that looking after others' cats was a missing service in Bath! Sue's subsequent investigations indicated such activity, underpinned by her love of cats, might be more viable than any other ideas we had previously explored for using our land. In the following years with much hard work she built up a very successful business.

View from the farm looking down over Bath

Tamasin and Darren during holiday in Ireland

Grandchildren Arthur and Polly

One man, his wife, and their dog Orson

Taking stock of everything led to a restructuring of the cattery staffing to free time up for Sue, and a building survey, after which we decided to add another room and improve a number of other areas. This turned out to be a major exercise and kept both Sue and I on our toes living with builders for months. On the family front, both Tamasin and Darren had by this time left home and started their careers. Tamasin studied theatre design at Central St Martin's and initially worked in London fringe theatre before shifting to her other great interest, ecology. Darren took a fine art degree at Wimbledon and, after some work in London, moved to be part of the contemporary arts scene in Glasgow.

On the professional front a number of people approached me asking if I would be interested in helping x y or z - but the first that came my way and really interested me was The Theatres Trust. I gladly accepted an invitation from the arts minister to chair this body. In many ways, of course, it was back to my first love, theatre buildings and it was also a follow-on from the building fabric study already under way. Peter Longman, the Trust's director, had given the organisation a different public profile than either of its first two directors Hugh Jenkins and John Earl, but to be fair it was only with the demise of the GLC that the Trust secured a reasonable income (when they were granted the freeholds of the Garrick, Lyric and Lyceum theatres; whilst the first two produce real income by way of rent the only revenue from the Lyceum derives from the sale of six seats per performance, not negligible for a hit musical of course).

The Trust met on a monthly basis and considered the Director's report on current business: working to preserve the nation's stock of theatre buildings past and present. The Theatres Trust had been established by Act of Parliament in 1976 to protect the nations' theatres but with little income and few powers. Any planning proposal affecting a theatre was supposed to be referred to the Trust, but it often fell to the Trust to remind local authorities of this requirement.

The report on the fabric of London's West End, *Act Now*, a legacy of that 2001 conference, was published in 2003, early on in my time with the Trust and whilst it didn't see government rushing to provide funds it did prompt some theatre managements to start refurbishment schemes and introduce ticket levies to fund them. Ed Mirvish had to an extent led the way with his complete refurbishment of the Old Vic in 1985. The most notable work in the West End came from Cameron Mackintosh who had been tempted into theatre ownership by Bernard Delfont and who, a while later, commissioned overall design schemes for his (Delfont Macintosh) theatres trying to recapture their original atmosphere while adding modern facilities. The majority of those schemes were from Clare Ferraby, the designer whom I had first met in connection with work on the Theatre Royal Nottingham for which her husband Nicholas Thompson was the senior planner. (Clare had at one stage been persuaded by me to do a preliminary colour scheme for the Coliseum exterior in Harewood's day). Cameron's work was followed by Lloyd-Webber's major work on Drury Lane in 2020. I am not sure either would cite the Trust's report as the reason for their work but they can be considered to have ploughed back some of their profits into the fabric which had helped generate a healthy income for them.

The Trust published – and still does - an annual publication highlighting theatres which were/are in some way at risk from development, demolition or lack of care. The inclusion of Adelina Patti's theatre at Craig y Nos in Wales for many years caused me much concern but try as we might it proved impossible to get any authority to stop the owner 'modernising' and creating hotel rooms out of the original dressing rooms as part of his B&B business – or stop the removal of understage structures to facilitate his 'ghost tours'. So much for its Grade 1 listing.

Our trustees were all experts in their fields. We were very lucky in my time to have those like Pat Thomas to provide guidance in planning law, Chris Shepley on how the planning inspectorate worked, Ron Spinney on how developers thought, as well as actors such as Simon Callow and Marilyn Cutts, who could explain what was needed for a building to work satisfactorily for performers. There was also the valuable input of theatre managers such as Sir Eddie Kulukundis, Sir Stephen Waley-Cohen, Genista Macintosh and Sam Shrouder as well as the MP Phyllis Starkey to give a steer on how her colleagues might be approached. Even if my fellow trustees weren't of the stature of earlier trustees such as Harold Wilson or Lord Goodman we offered a wide span of expertise and knowledge. We also recruited a new director when Peter Longman retired and, from a long list of candidates, chose Mhora Samuel who took the Trust further in several directions, especially by establishing an annual conference in 2007 thus creating a yearly opportunity to highlight issues of concern.

I served three terms on the Trust until 2009. Towards the end of my tenure the government decided that there should be more supervision of the recruitment of trustees and required such posts to be advertised and candidates to be interviewed. Penelope Keith treated her interview along the lines of an audition and provided much enjoyment.

When I retired from the Theatres Trust, Laurence Harbottle invited me to serve on the Peggy Ramsay Foundation. I never met this indomitable lady but had often seen her sweeping down St Martin's Lane from her office in Goodwins Court during my time at the Coliseum. In many ways Goodwins Court had been a major theatre centre at the time housing Theatre Projects and Eddie Kulukundis' Knightsbridge Productions. Ramsay was the most renowned theatrical agent of her time and when she died in 1991 her estate was left for those specifically writing for the stage. The foundation was established to help writers in as quick and unbureaucratic a way as possible – music to my ears after dealing with Arts Council forms for a period as a member of their stabilisation committee. (This was the Council's attempt to use some Lottery revenue to grant organisations cash to get out of particular difficulties. In other words a way around the fact that Lottery cash was only supposed to be for capital work!). I am not sure I contributed greatly to the Foundation meetings, dominated as they were by both serious and occasionally witty contributions from Michael Codron and David Hare, but I did at least persuade Brighton Council to name one of their buses after Peggy Ramsay as a former resident of the city!

There was one invitation that came in 2002 that I should have thought more about before accepting. This was an invitation from the Bristol Old Vic Trust to join their board. At that time BOV was not enjoying great success and was struggling to fill its 540 seats. Nevertheless, it was investigating the feasibility of building a new auditorium above the historic 18th century structure. I suppose I was swayed by the fact that I had a lot of nostalgia for the visits I had made to the BOV in my early days and forgot my father's comments that Bristolians were a funny lot (that's the polite version).

The basic aspirations of the organisation, quite distinct from the idea of an additional auditorium on the roof, were perfectly laudable in wanting to provide a more enjoyable physical experience in the historic auditorium to see work, and to make the front of house entrance from King Street more acceptable. Although the entrance had been transformed in the 70's from what I had known ten years earlier, the scheme by Peter Moro using the elegant Coopers' Hall next door as simply a grand staircase did nothing to entice visitors and wasted valuable space. Much discussion had already taken place about possible schemes by the time I joined the board and realised that the actual fabric was ultimately the responsibility of the Theatre Royal governors, a separate entity. Add to this the fact that the BOV did not have an artistic director as such (they seemed to have drawn blanks with recruitment) and that some of the board had been *in situ* for over ten years, it will be realised that I should perhaps not have accepted the invitation so readily.

But accept the invitation I did, and mistakenly agreed to take on the chair when proposed by Simon Relph (a board member whom I had known from Coliseum days when he was the technical boss at the National), this after David Sproxton (a senior member of the Aardman Animations company of Wallace and Gromit fame) had resigned. We did then attract as joint artistic directors what we considered a pair with exciting ideas for the organisation, Simon Reade and David Farr. Although they rubbed up a number of people the wrong way, especially the theatre's governors, with their removal of reminders of past glories from around the foyers, they did produce interesting work. Indeed, in 2006 the *Daily Telegraph* could record *"Apologies for the déjà vu you're bound to experience in reading that Bristol Old Vic has, once again, excelled itself."*

Unfortunately, David was tempted by an offer from the RSC and left the partnership quite soon after. Simon's skills were as more of a dramaturg and attendances dropped for his programme. As the plans for alterations had reached the stage where they could form the basis of an appeal for funds, the BOV board, faced with dire warnings from the Arts Council of grant withdrawal, decided that the theatre should close in 2007 while the plans for rebuilding were acted on. Shock horror and cries of outrage from many who didn't bother to get the facts straight. There was a general misconception that the theatre retained a permanent company of actors (as had been the case in the 50s and 60s) and that these would now all be thrown out of work. In reality, companies were actually assembled anew for each production, as was the norm with most regional producing houses at this time. Although the closure decision had been given unanimous approval by the board, when I resigned it somehow appeared that it was mostly my fault. As Tim West put it at my Theatres Trust retirement reception "Well, you can't win them all".

After the Bristol experience I wasn't keen to give up time for further ventures but one from Cardiff came my way that I thought might be fun.

With the growing reputation of the UK as a seat of musicals there had been a move to celebrate the fact with a festival of some kind. This led to the 'Quest for New Musicals', a national competition culminating in a 5-day event at Buxton Opera House in 1992 (the brainchild of Chris Grady working in the Mackintosh office and later for SOLT on various promotions). The Quest initiative led to an organisation being formed in Cardiff initially at the time the city was bidding for cultural capital status to create a regular festival of musicals. Jo Benjamin, a widely experienced general manager of West End musicals, especially for Michael White, had become involved as Chief Executive. It was originally 'The International Festival of Musical Theatre in Cardiff' but the board insisted on changing this to 'The Cardiff International Festival of Musical Theatre' after the first Festival in 2002; such were local politics!

Jo suggested to her board that they might benefit from my expertise. Brian Rix was already involved but there was no one else with theatre background. The board was chaired by Vincent Kane OBE whose broadcasting background had earned him (to some) the description of the Welsh Jeremy Paxman. The aim was to present a selection of great musicals around the already well-established BBC Cardiff Singer of the World competition and benefit from associated publicity. Unfortunately, this never really took off and despite Jo's energy and extensive contacts in the world of musicals - Gary Wilmot, Clive Rowe and Ruthie Henshall were all involved in a gala concert as part of the first festival - it failed to gain the necessary financial support. Nonetheless, an interesting series of meetings and three notable festivals.

By 2011 I had spent a lot of time reading papers and attending meetings of arts bodies and decided to take more interest in a society I had joined early in retirement, the Frank Matcham Society. This was a body dedicated to promoting an appreciation of the great Victorian theatre architect responsible for the building where I had spent almost twenty years of my professional life – as well as over 90 splendid others. Since becoming a member I had attended a number of meetings, joined several theatre-visiting trips both abroad and in the UK, and met up with a number of former colleagues and like-minded individuals. Roger Lobb had been a member for some while together with Tony Mabbutt, whom I had vaguely known as the Royal Opera House box office manager in my Coliseum days. New acquaintances included the former dancer Gerry Atkins, who had managed his own troupe for many years. As a group we found that we had much in common and often enjoyed meals together. I was happy, therefore, to take on the role of chairman when these colleagues made the suggestion. My predecessor had tended to fix a programme of visits around the shows he wished to see and didn't realise you couldn't just turn up unannounced at a stage door and expect to be shown around a busy theatre building, especially when accompanied by several others, all intent on photographing every nook and cranny of the building. I was elected chairman at the AGM in Liverpool in 2011 and set about arranging tours at home and in Europe using my various contacts.

Our first tour took in Amsterdam, the Hague and Leiden in Holland. We were given extensive tours of both old and new buildings and walked many miles. There followed tours to Copenhagen and the delightful theatres in The Marche in Italy (which, in all the holidays Sue and I had spent touring in Italy, we had never reached). I also arranged a tour to Germany and from the various theatres in Munich progressed via Bayreuth to marvel at the Semperoper in Dresden and the small but fascinating theatre at Kochberg with its Goethe connections .

Besides these overseas trips I arranged tours of several theatres, by Matcham and others, around the UK. After five years I felt I had brought a little more organisation to the society and established a more professional body than it had been: I had added a Journal to the society's publications and brought more profile with a short film and a lunch celebrating Matcham's 150th anniversary at the transformed Hippodrome in Leicester Square. Time to move on and I felt the society's future would be in safe hands when I passed the chair (via a democratic election of course!) to Mark Fox who I had recruited as a member.

One further body has attracted my interest in 'retirement' - the Association of Historic Theatres in Europe, 'Perspectiv'. I first learnt of this body from a conversation with Mhora Samuel at the Theatres Trust when she explained there was a project being organised by the association to link up historic theatres in Europe and promote visiting them by advertising their existence on literature as 'European Routes of Historic Theatres'. The project was funded by a grant from the EU's Cultural Fund and also involved cooperation between six theatre museums to produce an exhibition, 'The History of Europe Told by its Theatres'. This was first shown in public at a conference in Warsaw and I thought brought a new way of appreciating the role of theatre buildings in our history. I was not so sure about the 'Routes' project but I have certainly benefitted from the collection of concise information the leaflets have provided. The organisation behind these two projects was founded in Germany in 2002 and its highly detailed constitution certainly reflected its Teutonic origin.

Once again, as a result of perhaps saying too much, I found myself on the board and subsequently lived through the experience of both spending EU funds and accounting for them. In 2019 I even attended a meeting of members from around the Black Sea in Chernivitsi in the Ukraine. My last participation as a board member was at the 2022 conference in Sabionetta, brilliantly hosted by the local council and their dedicated official, Cristina Valenti.

TIME FOR REFLECTION

· ·

Sunset at Honeysuckle Farm

When I began this journey down memory lane I commented on having experienced an interesting life. It has certainly been that but as I have reviewed the highs and lows of some eighty years and those I have met who have come into my life it has struck me that I have been privileged to know as bosses, colleagues, friends and acquaintances many people who have made my life that much richer for their contact.

Olivier, Arlen, Harewood, Goodman, the Hochhausers - all stand out as people I never dreamed of meeting as I struggled in that Aldwych box office. But these are only a few of the personalities who have played a part in my professional life. Theatre can be all-consuming to the extent of dominating all of the twenty-four hours in the day - but it certainly brings rich rewards in the family it makes. I would still commend a life in arts management but I fear that now it would be a different kind of life to that I have experienced and, I suspect, offer less enjoyment.

I have also seen organisations change – some such as those of the funding system – out of all recognition. When I first became aware of its existence the Arts Council (then of Great Britain) was run by those who had worked at the coal face in some way. Now it is operated – at government's behest – by those who see their jobs as ensuring government policy and beliefs are complied with before public money is released. We may have been relaxed in the 60s but have we gone too far the other way?

Theatre companies have also changed and I cannot but help thinking that I worked for ENO in its heyday, a feeling reinforced as I write by the Arts Council's major reduction in funding and relocation proposal. I see no evidence of the decline of 'grand opera' as the Council's Music Director apparently does.

The world moves on and it would be wrong to dismiss significant progress in recognition of sexual equality and orientation. Little did I realise when visiting my Magdalen colleague Danny Wolfenden at his father's vice chancellor's residence in Reading during our Oxford days in the early sixties, what changes his father's later report would bring. It was a real privilege to have heard Arthur Mitchell encourage his company to strive for absolute excellence in spite of (or perhaps because of) the challenges then facing black dancers.

I have witnessed the theatre world revolutionised by happenings at the Royal Court from *Look Back In Anger* onwards, and musicals progress from American imports to the home-grown spectaculars of Lloyd Webber and Cameron Mackintosh.

There have of course been changes that I never dreamt of in those days at the Aldwych box office even when fantasising about how computers would change the world. They certainly have. When I despair of being asked to choose option x or y by a mechanical voice rather than a human after ringing a number, I remind myself of the frustration of listening to a phone ringing unanswered in the past when calling a box office. And did I really believe that one day a computer would give me a view of the stage from the seat I was planning to buy? Perhaps.

Yes, I did believe in evolution rather than revolution when steering the affairs of theatre leaders and I believe that in some small way this brought about significant change.

And now, having belatedly followed my Latin master's exhortation to my schoolboy self and written things down in this Vade Mecum, I shall draw these rather rambling memories to a close. It has certainly been an interesting exercise to try and capture in some way on paper a little of what has undoubtedly been an enjoyable and challenging life.

I would not have achieved this record of forty years without the help of many people; I thank first of all Rosy Runciman who regularly repeated - but more politely - in my early retirement days, the exhortation of my Latin master, to "write it down". To do just that I have been fortunate in having considerable help from my former colleague, Paul James. To all those who have responded to searching questions about the past, some who sadly are no longer around, I am very grateful and hope I have not made too many errors.

The record would be poorer without the images I have included, many coming from the stock of Chris Arthur, a great photographer and friend of many years' standing. For others I record thanks even if I have been unable to trace their source.

Life in theatre can be all demanding and my family has certainly allowed me to respond to its calls and I thank them profusely for allowing me do so.

Rupert Rhymes, 2023